What is "TIME-OUT?"

- It's the effective new way of combining communication, love and positive reinforcement to solve repeated misbehavior in children from 2 to 6 years old . . .

- It was developed by one of America's most prominent pediatric psychologists in response to parents who found that the traditional methods of discipline and punishment weren't working for them . . .

- It can be used to effectively teach a child both the rules of the family and the rules of society—while at the same time nurturing his feelings of self-esteem . . .

- It's a method that will help you through the short-term crisis of the moment AND will bring about positive changes in your child's behavior and attitude over the long-term . . .

- It's the one approach that works . . . AFTER ALL OTHER APPROACHES HAVE FAILED:

  Discover how parents who once had problems with their young children have solved them—thanks to Dr. James W. Varni's unique program:

TIME-OUT FOR TODDLERS

Berkley Books by Dr. James W. Varni and Donna G. Corwin

TIME OUT FOR TODDLERS
GROWING UP GREAT

TIME-OUT FOR TODDLERS

Positive Solutions to Typical Problems in Children

Dr. James W. Varni and Donna G. Corwin

BERKLEY BOOKS, NEW YORK

TIME-OUT FOR TODDLERS

A Berkley Book / published in association with
Stan Corwin Productions

PRINTING HISTORY
Berkley trade paperback edition / September 1991

The Penguin Putnam Inc. World Wide Web site address is
http://www.penguinputnam.com

ISBN: 0-425-12943-8

BERKLEY®
Berkley Books are published by The Berkley Publishing Group,
a division of Penguin Putnam Inc.,
375 Hudson Street, New York, New York 10014.
BERKLEY and the "B" design
are trademarks belonging to Penguin Putnam Inc.

PRINTED IN THE UNITED STATES OF AMERICA

20   19   18   17

Acknowledgments

We want to gratefully acknowledge and thank those people whose help and support made this book possible.

Roger Cooper, Publisher, Berkley Books, who believed in us from the beginning and who will soon be using "Time-Out" with his own toddler.

Trish Todd and **Hillary Cige**, our editors at Berkley, a "special" thank you.

Judith Madison and **Shirley Gram**, who shared so much of themselves and their experiences with their children.

Stan Corwin, who acted as our guide, editor, agent, mentor, friend, and relative. Thank you.

Ann Benya, thank you for your flying fingers on the keyboard.

And thank you to the **parents** everywhere who use "Time-Out" and help us all.

To the Children
—James Walter Varni

To my precious Alexandra, a "Time-Out" trooper
and
To my husband, Stan
—Donna Gelgur Corwin

Contents

Contents

Introduction

Dr. James W. Varni

This book is the result of years of clinical practice during which many of the families who were referred to me by local pediatricians had very similar concerns—that is, how to handle the common behavior problems of young children, typically between two and one half and ten years of age. After seeing that so often these parents desperately needed a forum and some direction to help with their children's **normal** behavior problems, I decided to conduct parent's groups. I used a variety of different discipline methods, but "Time-Out" was the single most effective technique used by parents over the years.

Eventually, the overwhelmingly positive response resulted in the realization that presenting these powerful techniques in a clear and understandable parent-oriented book would make it available to a greater number of families. It is important to point out that this realization was precipitated by Donna Corwin (coauthor), who was a parent of a three-year-old at the time (taking my parent's group course). She suggested that, given how successful the time-out chair was working for her family and other families in the group, a book delineating these techniques would be useful for a large number of parents. Actually, I think she used the words "help" and "lifesaver." This book was born out of that success.

In conducting these parent's groups it became evident that parents needed clear, to-the-point, focused information, as well as written outlines in checklist form on how to deal with **common everyday behavior problems**. This is what this book will present.

The parent question-and-answer chapter is not taken from theoretical data. It comes partly from the head; mostly from the heart. The case examples are composites of the many families I have worked with in my clinical practice. Every parent should find himself or herself in our chapters at least once, but probably a lot more. Please be certain to read the case studies and questions-and-answers chapters carefully. They will serve as your own personal consultant on how to use "Time-Out" correctly.

It helps to know other parents are feeling and experiencing the exact same things you are. *Time-Out for Toddlers* will become a friend to you. I suspect you will refer to it often. I also suspect that you will share it with friends—parents who have children the same age as yours. This is exactly what has happened in my clinical practice—parents share with other parents what one parent has termed "an eloquently simple technique!" One, by the way, that works!

It is essential to recognize from the beginning that "Time-Out" does **not** involve yelling, screaming, or hitting. **Frequent use of "Time-Out" will not break your child's spirit!** In fact, using "Time-Out" often will keep you from **having to yell** at your child in order to try to gain compliance. Yelling is emotionally destructive to your child. Consequently, by using "Time-Out" as the primary form of discipline, in combination with lots of love and no yelling, you will find that your child's self-esteem and positive feelings of self-worth will be enhanced. By reading *Time-Out for Toddlers* you will learn how to correctly combine your love, praise, and positive attention with "Time-Out;" as a result, you will be a more effective parent, and your child will be happier and healthier emotionally.

Introduction

Donna G. Corwin

Before I had a child, the only things that mattered in my life were my husband and my writing. They were both reasonable and manageable most of the time. Then I became a parent and life as I knew it was changed forever. I eat, sleep, and have anxiety attacks over my four-year-old daughter, precious Alexandra. I've been told my frustrations are normal. But if this is normal, I feel for those parents who are really neurotic.

She gooed and gurgled her way into my heart; an easy baby, sweet, funny, and a great sleeper. Then she learned how to walk, how to talk, how to manipulate, whine, and say the big **NO!**

From that moment on the tears started. But they weren't her tears, they were MINE. No one ever prepared me how to handle a strong-willed, independent, temperamental child. I was fearful of raising a brat. On the other hand, I didn't envision myself spanking her ten times a day. It was much too *Mommie Dearest* for me. I also needed a form of discipline that would work for my husband, my housekeeper, and any other caregiver who needed some control in my absence, and in my presence.

I read the experts from Spock to Bettelheim. Their advice was long, drawn-out, often outdated, and theoretical. Some of the information was useful but did not account for different situations. What I wanted was a step-by-step, simple method of discipline that made sense. Don't give me long explanations **why**. TELL ME HOW. Most of my friends seemed to feel much the same way I did. Although the term "Time-Out" was floating around in our vocabulary, no one really understood how to implement it properly.

Then one day, my friend Judith saw a flier in her young son's pediatrician's office for a parents' group given by Dr. James Varni. When it said that he dealt with discipline, I canceled my dinner plans and went along. Although he offered to talk about almost any topic relating to children, the women who showed up all had toddlers, and they all wanted to talk about discipline. And talk and talk and talk.

We discussed our successes and our struggles with "Time-Out" and our children's progress. I discovered it is not a "one-shot" wonder method. "Time-Out," like all behavioral changes, takes **time** and **effort**. You have to be patient, consistent, and willing to follow through. If you do, **I guarantee it works**.

I almost gave up the fight numerous times. There was a myriad of excuses. I was too tired. We were in an inconvenient place. Alexandra would embarrass me. My husband said to "let it go." So we slipped back into disciplinary hell. Dr. Varni was always a phone call away. He led us through the "Time-Out" method over and over again. He made me keep trying.

Then one day my daughter would not listen. She was obstinate and out of control. I called, "Time-Out." I had to drag her to the "Time-Out" chair, but I didn't back down. She cried. She screamed. But she SAT! For three long, quiet minutes. The timer dinged. "Can I get up now, Mommy?" "Yes," I said. "I'm sorry, Mommy," she whispered, as she hugged and kissed me. "OK, Alexandra. 'Time-Out' is over." "I love you," she said. "Me, too," I replied.

A **BREAKTHROUGH**. It worked! I used "Time-Out" three more times that day. I've used it many, many times since. Alexandra IS NOT the perfect child. She's still a hell-raiser. But she understands the rules. Suddenly her actions have a cause and effect. She has boundaries.

Dr. Varni believes that "Time-Out" gives children a sense of security. I agree. I cannot think of a more important book to help parents in their struggle in raising a child.

Discipline is the number-one topic that parents talk about. There are many schools of thought. But if you can discipline your child so both of you maintain your sense of respect, so you don't physically or mentally harm your child or leave the child feeling fearful, then I can't imagine why Dr. Varni's "Time-Out" wouldn't be the only form of discipline a parent would ever use for her young child. I also can't imagine what my life would be like without his incredible method. My husband compares the "Five Steps" to time-out in sports. He says it gives you a chance to regroup and rethink the situation.

How simple! How ingenious! I look forward to sharing *Time-Out for Toddlers* with other parents. Especially those parents who, out of frustration, may have turned to spanking and yelling. I wish my parents could have had this book. I know my children will.

1

"Every Four Minutes . . ."

Can you imagine spanking or yelling at your child every few minutes? If you think that sounds outrageous, think again. Research has shown that mothers of preschoolers respond to their children at the rate of once every four minutes!

Behavior problems are normal. Let's understand that right from the beginning. Every childhood stage goes through what is termed "age-appropriate behavior." If a toddler lies down on the floor periodically and has a crying, screaming tantrum, that is **normal**. If a ten-year-old displays the same behavior, then it's time to talk.

Too many parents worry that their children are abnormal if they display undesirable behavior. Husbands and wives start to blame each other, their weird Uncle Harold, or society in general.

One of the mothers from Dr. Varni's parent's

group was almost hysterical because her three-year-old woke up in the middle of the night yelling, whining, and screaming. She described her little girl's behavior as abnormal and was ready to take her to therapy.

Dr. Varni asked the mother to "problem solve" (think out what may have led to her child's behavior). He asked what her day had been like. He discovered that she had spent her time taking her daughter from one birthday party to another. The child consumed at least two ice-cream cones, three pieces of cake, Cokes, candy, chocolates, potato chips, and punch. She was overstimulated and excited. Even the most placid toddler would have been jumping off the walls with that much sugar rushing through her little body.

The distraught mother was elated after her simple discovery. She realized one night's aberration was not directly related to her daughter's psychological development.

There is a very good reason why mothers of preschoolers respond to their children's behavior at the rate of once every four minutes. Children who are seven years of age or younger are at the "preabstract level of cognitive development," which means they are unable to deal with abstractions, such as reasoning. If a parent tells her three-year-old daughter, Amy, not to go into the street because there are cars and she might get hit and be hurt, Amy may be perfectly capable of repeating such an instruction back to her mom and dad, but that is where her ability ends. It is extremely unlikely that she will be able to actually do what her parent instructs her to do.

Because reasoning with young children doesn't work, it usually results in repeating the instruction over and over again, and using threats and nagging, such as, "If I have to tell you one more time," or, "If I've told you once, I've told you a hundred times." Her parents end up telling her the same thing over and over again because Amy is unable to comply with the instruction, due to her level of cognitive development. When Mom has to repeat the instruction continually, she may begin to believe that Amy is openly defying her, and Mom begins to feel frustrated and/or angry. Amy, unable to comply, begins to feel that Mom does not love her. Over time, repeated attempts to reason with a child can result in lowering the child's self-esteem. As this coercive process goes on, day after day, the parent gets more and more frustrated, and the child develops a very poor self-image.

Children learn through repetition. Children must have the opportunity to practice the same thing over and over again. If Amy needs to be taught not to go into the street, she must be shown this lesson over and over again. Every time that Amy goes near the street, she needs to be disciplined, in an unemotional way. Every time that she starts to go toward the street but stops short of doing so, she needs to be praised. After Amy has experienced 20 or 30 trips toward the street, with some resulting in discipline and some in praise, she will learn from the contrast to stay out of the street.

Parents cannot tell small children ONCE not to do something and realistically expect the child never to do it again. Parents need to understand that teaching involves many repetitions before something is learned and that children must do something both the right way and the wrong way many times before they learn to do it right consistently. Rather than becoming frustrated because learning takes place over a long period of time, parents should understand that they are in the process of teaching their child an important skill. The more times the child can experience the contrast between what happens when something is done the right way and when it is done the wrong way, the quicker and more thoroughly the child will learn what the right way is.

You are reading this book because you care, because your method of discipline doesn't feel quite right, and you need a new direction.

If you want to chart your child's behavior pattern on a graph to see if it falls in the normal range, chances are you won't be able to. Personalities are different. People are different. Although there are some basic similarities that are age appropriate, no two children behave exactly alike.

What's age appropriate? Children develop at different physical and psychological rates. Not every child walks at ten months or talks at a year.

Some parents put unrealistic expectations on their children because they simply don't know what's *age appropriate* for their child. If you feel your three-year-old should be brushing her own teeth and you get into battles over this issue, then maybe you should problem solve to make sure you're not asking **too** much of her.

- Ask other parents (at least three or four) if their children brush their own teeth regularly without any parental help.

- Ask your pediatrician about age-appropriate behavior for certain tasks.

- Watch your child. If she seems unable to master a skill and continually complains because she is frustrated, then observe and listen and rethink your expectations.

- Use constant encouragement and reinforcement when your child is trying to master a new skill. If you use positive reinforcement, the child will be more apt to want to manage a skill on her own.

Toddler Checks and Balances Checklist

1. Observe your child at play.
2. Talk to friends who have children the same age. Ask them about their child's behavior. You'll be surprised to hear their stories.
3. Watch your child in toddler groups or at school.
4. Talk to your child's group leader or teacher.
5. Observe **other** children.
6. Join a parent's group.
7. Read and use this book often.

If after you've followed our suggestions you still feel your child has a problem or you have doubts about her behavior, seek out a qualified pediatric psychologist or confer with your pediatrician.

PROBLEM SOLVING

Parents often report that they have used "Time-Out" in the past, and it didn't work. Dr. Varni discovered in his clinical practice that almost 100 percent of the time parents were **not using "Time-Out" correctly**. That is, they were using what they **thought** was "Time-Out" but, in practice, they did not follow the proven steps that make "Time-Out" work so effectively. When parents follow the steps we will subsequently describe, we "guarantee" that with the vast **majority**, "Time-Out" will reduce the common behavior problems of toddlerhood. This method can make the difference between totally enjoying your child or forcing the constant battle of wills that often makes ages two to five so notorious and unpleasant.

The overall Parents' Five-Step Problem-solving Program for using "Time-Out" can make the difference between an effective parent and the victim of a defiant child.

Step 1: Mind-set

Having a rational, realistic, and positive attitude about your child's behavior problems goes a long way toward effectively managing her. The next time you encounter a behavior problem, remember the following ideas:

- Behavior problems are **common to all young children**. If your child misbehaves, that means she is normal!

- Many parents face similar behavior problems. You are **not** alone!

- It is **not** catastrophic or awful when your child misbehaves. It's part of growing up!

- Do **not** avoid dealing with a behavior problem at the time it occurs. It is better to attempt to solve it right then, not later!

- It is best to **stop and think** before solving a behavior problem. Ask yourself, "What is it I have to do to manage this behavior problem?"

- You **can** manage behavior problems! These problems are solvable if you correctly use the behavior-modification techniques described in this book.

Step 2: Problem Identification and Definition

Before you modify or change your child's behavior, you must define "the problem" in a concrete manner. Descriptions such as "bad attitude," "defiant," "strong-willed" are not specific enough for you to begin the process of being an effective user of "Time-Out." More useful descriptions are: "refused to pick up her toys within ten seconds after I asked her to do so"; "gets up every night and comes into my bed"; "hits her younger sister." Determine the *who, what, where, when, why,* and *how* of the behavior problem.

Step 3: Alternative Solutions

This step requires brainstorming toward a solution. Parents need to mentally generate a list of ways to modify their child's behavior. "Time-Out" is often the most effective technique, but for some behavior problems, such as separation anxiety, other behavioral techniques described in this book will be needed.

Step 4: Decision Making

Consider the following when making a decision—

- What is the likelihood that this choice will reduce my child's behavior problem?

- What is the likelihood that I can implement this solution in its optimal form?

It is always best to combine discipline techniques such as "Time-Out" with a lot of praise and reinforcement for appropriate behavior. Thus, when deciding on which techniques to use, always remember to try to praise your child when she is being good, don't just discipline her when she is misbehaving.

Step 5: Solution Implementation and Verification

Having decided on which behavioral technique to use, you next need to try it out and evaluate its effectiveness. If the technique is effective in changing your child's behavior in the desired direction, congratulations! You are parenting effectively. On the other hand, if your child's behavior does not change, then two reasons are possible: 1) You chose the incorrect behavioral technique, and you need to go back to your mental checklist and select the next one on the list; or 2) You implemented the behavioral technique incorrectly.

In the following sections of this book we will provide detailed behavioral guidelines that describe **how** to use "Time-Out" and other behavior modification techniques, **when** to use other techniques, and **where** to use "Time-Out." When "Time-Out" does not work, it is inevitably because some common mistakes are being made. We will list the most frequent mistakes that parents make when using "Time-Out." You'll be on your way to an incredible new experience as your child's behavior becomes more manageable and pleasant.

2

"Time for Toddlers"

A three-year-old sat quietly playing with her doll for more than 30 minutes. Her mom said to herself, "Thank God, she's quiet at last!" and ignored her the whole 30 minutes. Then suddenly, her daughter flung her doll across the room. The doll's head hit the wall and fell off. The little girl started to cry. Her mother came running in. "What happened?" inquired her mom. The little girl held up the headless doll. "I want to play with *you*, Mommy, not my dolly."

"CATCH 'EM BEING GOOD"

Young children are so used to the words "no," "you can't," and "don't" that positive reinforcement is often not even a part of their understandable vocabulary. It is vitally important to praise good behavior. Children, like adults, need praise and parental attention, a pat on the back, a smile, a kiss, and a hug just for playing nicely. All these positive gestures reinforce desired behavior.

The more time you spend on **acceptable behavior**, the less time you will inevitably spend on punishment. Most children crave attention, so it makes sense that positive attention for good behavior **and** negative attention for problem behavior will both effectively increase behavior. Children will act out to receive even negative attention; it is a lot better than being ignored!

When you "catch your child being good," you are teaching him how to behave. Eventually, your child will learn how to exhibit socially acceptable behavior and will be able to gain praise from peers, teachers, relatives, and most importantly, you.

What's key is to catch children's good behavior *often*. Use physical contact *many* times a day. Touch his shoulders, pat his head, give him a quick kiss. Try not to interrupt the natural flow of his play. Don't stop and give your child a long dissertation about his good behavior. Toddlers are to the point little beings. Say what you have to say and move on.

It's important not to overreact when children misbehave. They will then look for attention any way they can get it.

As they watch your temper escalating, they'll feel powerful in knowing they're driving you crazy. Having some control over parental behavior can be very reinforcing for young children, who generally do not have control over major aspects of their lives.

By their very nature, infants require a lot of physical contact from their parents. As children get older, parents usually touch them much less, because children are more independent and usually do not want to be touched as often. By the time they turn four, they are usually toilet trained, can get dressed and undressed without help, and can feed and bathe themselves. Thus, if parents don't consciously make an effort to give hugs and kisses and touch their child, he or she will be touched much less than they were at earlier ages. There are several things that parents can do to help offset these natural changes:

1. "Child Close"—During playtimes or TV time, sit close to your child. Do the same when you are in a restaurant, shopping, or just walking with your child. You want to be close enough to give reassurance if needed.

2. "Reach Out and Touch"—Touch your child as often as possible each day—even for a few seconds—but don't smother your toddler. They'll tend to push you away—just a touch, not a bear hug, will let them know how you feel.

3. "If You Don't Have Anything Nice to Say . . ."—Children don't have the advanced verbal skills that adults do. Adults often send messages that are misunderstood by children, who may interpret verbal reprimands, nagging, and yelling as signs that their parents do not love them. Think before you speak harshly to your child. Your words may end up

having a negative effect such as low self-esteem.

4. "The No-Talk Touch"—Too much talking can be distracting, especially if a child is preoccupied with an enjoyable activity. A smile can soothe your child without unnecessarily disrupting his play.

POSITIVE-PERFORMANCE PROGRAM

"Catch 'Em Being Good" involves learning how to spend positive time with your child without yelling, getting angry, or pushing each other's buttons. Learning how to play with your child is not always easy. The following steps will help you to set up a positive program for your child's good behavior and establish a loving, bonded relationship. Remember, every time you catch your child being good, it builds a good self-image.

1. Choose a time of day, either after school or after dinner, if your child is school-age. For preschoolers, the morning is best. Set aside about ten minutes for younger children and about 20 minutes for an older child. This will be your "special" time together.

2. Try to spend time together at least five times the first week. After that, set aside at least three times a week. Make this part of your lives together.

3. *Do not* involve any other children in this play period! Do not talk on the phone or plan any

other activities. Make sure no one disturbs you and your child.

4. Ask your child what he would like to do (excluding watching television). Be open and let him choose the activity. If he wants to act like doggies, be a good sport and go along with it. You'll be surprised by your child's wonderful imagination.

5. Join in as your child plays. Talk about what he's doing. Be enthusiastic.

6. *Do not* question or give directions. This will disrupt your child's play. *Do not* teach your child anything during the playtime. This is *strictly* a time to enjoy each other's company.

7. Use *positive* praise and approval of your child's use of imagination, creativity, intelligence, and fun.

CHILD'S COMPLIANCE

It is not easy to get young children to comply with our wishes. That's why it is so important to start early to get children to follow your requests. When you ask your child to do something, give your child **immediate** feedback on how well she is listening. As soon as you make your request and your child begins to comply, immediately praise your child for complying, as in: "Mommy likes it when you do what I ask," "Good listening!" "Nice manners."

You cannot give too much praise. Kids eat it up like ice cream! Use any words that specifically relay to your child that you appreciate that he is doing what was asked of him. If your little one has done a job or chore on his own initiative, this is the time to provide "extra extra praise." You may even want to give your child a surprise. This will help your child remember and follow household rules and jobs without always being told to do so.

Be nice when you ask your child to do something. Choose two or three commands your child follows inconsistently or not at all. Make a special effort to praise your child whenever he or she listens and obeys the particular requests.

During the next few weeks take a few minutes each day and work with your child. Select a time when your child is not very busy and ask him or her to do very brief favors for you such as, "Please hand me a towel/spoon/magazine/and so on." Don't choose a task that's too difficult. Give about two or three of these in a row during these few minutes. As your child follows each one, be sure to provide specific praise for your child's compliance. This will result in your child giving his best effort to win your praise.

Try to have several of these compliance sessions daily. This provides an excellent opportunity to **catch your child being good**. Plus, it will make your life easier.

Key Points to Remember About Teaching Compliance

1. Make certain that you have your child's attention; get eye contact!

2. Make your requests *short* and to the *point*.

3. Do not make multiple requests. It's confusing.

4. Make sure you are clearly understood.

5. Let the request sink in, and give a little time (ten seconds) for your child to comply.

6. Don't wait too long to praise or reward your child. If he's listened to your request, go for it!

7. If your child doesn't comply, immediately use "Time-Out" or take away privileges.

8. During the first few "training" days, make at least three simple requests per day. The better your child listens, the more requests you can make.

9. Arguing and false threats will waste your time and set you back. It's important to be consistent and follow through!

HOW TO "MAKE 'EM GOOD BEFORE THEY'RE BAD"

Susan, a working mom, was negotiating a big real-estate deal over the telephone. Her three-year-old, Kevin, screamed into the phone, "Mommy, take me pee-pee." Susan excused herself and quickly ran to help Kevin in the bathroom and then returned to the phone. Kevin decided to give a concert and began singing and banging a tambourine. She told him to leave the room. He started to whine and cry. Again Susan excused herself. After five interruptions, the frustrated client said he'd talk to her another time. Susan lost the deal to another agent who responded more quickly.

Parents can go into social abstinence when they have toddlers for fear the child will totally disrupt their business or social lives at home. This should not be the case. Children should be aware of rules that they are to follow when Mom or Dad is talking on the phone or has guests over.

Part of the immediate problem is that parents provide too much attention to a disruptive child. The following guidelines will help establish ground rules:

1. If you have to make a telephone call or the phone rings and you want to talk, tell your child that "Mommy is talking on the telephone" and that he should not disturb you. Give your child an activity. Tell him to go play in his room, watch television, or go quietly into the next room and play. BE DIRECT.

2. If your child manages not to bother you during the entire time you are engaged, provide EXTRA praise. These same methods should be used when you have company visiting. It is important that you state what the rules and expectations are before your guests arrive. If your child disrupts your guests, do not be timid about putting him in "Time-Out." Children will often test us to see if we will follow through when we have company over. Your toddler may be in for a BIG surprise. Try a "practice" run for a week or so until your child understands. Call a friend or have someone

over who has children and understands what you are attempting to accomplish. You can even pretend to be talking to someone on the phone if you feel uncomfortable about subjecting a friend to what you're afraid will be an experiment in frustration.

Praise and Attention

We have stressed how important it is to give praise on a continuing basis to build your child's self-esteem and reinforce good behavior. But there are some key points regarding praise and attention that parents should use to both their child's and their own best advantage.

- Be sincere.
- Use physical affection when you praise your child (hugs, kisses, pats, and so on).
- Withhold praise and attention when your child misbehaves.
- Be specific about what you praise. Example: "Mommy likes it when you pick up your toys."
- Remember to praise even the small "good" behavior that your child does.
- Don't pay attention to minor annoying behavior.

Key Points to Remember About Rewards and Privileges

- Give rewards and privileges **only after** your child complies with a request or does something appropriate on his own without being told to.

- Don't give a new bicycle if your little one brushes his teeth two days in a row. Keep the reward in proportion to the deed.

- Keep up the positive praise. For example, "This is because you listened so well!"

- Rewards are not always material. Getting to help with the dishes, washing the car with Daddy, or going to the park serve as excellent reinforcers.

- Don't just pick a reward **you like**. Make sure it will make your child happy.

You already do many things for your child (whether or not they behave) like reading stories, cooking his favorite foods, letting him watch a video, or even giving him an allowance. These freebies can be made contingent on your child's appropriate behavior. Use all of the everyday nice things you do for your child as reinforcers for good behavior.

All of these behaviors, praise, rewards, privileges are part of the socialization process used in conjunction with "Time-Out." They reinforce positive behavior and help you to **catch your child being good**. This is the key point. Don't focus only on problem behavior, think about all the things you can do to encourage good behavior.

Too many parents are waiting around for their child to misbehave. Expect the best and you won't get the worst. All of these methods build higher self-esteem. These positive methods will also give a child better coping skills. As children learn to deal with problems and difficult situations, they are less frustrated and angry. Thus, they are apt to display better behavior because they feel good about themselves and their ability to work out a difficult situation.

Key Points to Remember About Ignoring Minor Misbehavior

- Use "ignoring" whenever your child does a **minor** misbehavior that seems to be an attempt to get your attention.

- Use "ignoring" *each time* the misbehavior occurs.

- When you ignore a misbehavior, it may get worse before it gets better.

- If the misbehavior becomes too difficult to avoid attending to, it is time to use the "Time-Out" procedure described in the next chapter.

- Ignoring means no attention of any kind. No glaring, no staring, no scolding, no explanations, no finger pointing. **No attention!**

- Don't start to ignore and then give in. This will only teach your child to keep up his misbehavior for a longer period of time in order to get your attention.

- Counting to ten, watching TV, reading, calling a friend, or walking out of the room will help you to ignore minor misbehavior. Always pay attention to incompatible behavior. For example, if your child continually leaves his dirty plates on the table when he is finished eating, strongly praise him when he remembers to take his plate to the sink.

Examples of Social Reinforcement
Verbal

I like it when you _____. (clean your room, eat quickly, help me without being asked, play so quietly)

That's a great _____. (tower, fort, game, picture)

You're really doing a good job of _____. (helping me, baking that cake, sawing that wood, building the model)

Those ____ are really ____. (cookies, colors; good, pretty)

You're doing just what I asked and so _____. (quickly, fast, neatly, happily)

I like the way you _____. (helped Mommy today, took care of your sister, played without fighting with your friends)

The way you are ____ is really great. (working hard at your homework)

That's (pointing) _____. (great, really pretty, good, carefully done)

I really like (enjoy) ____ with you. (playing, shopping, working)

You can really pick interesting (fun) ____. (ways to keep busy, games to play, things to do)

I like how you are _____; that's so _____. (cleaning, coloring, making your bed; nice, pretty, helpful)

You're doing such a ____ job; that's ____ than I could do! (careful, neat; better, nicer)

Physical
Ruffle hair
Gently squeeze arm
Pat on head, back, hand
Hug
Kiss

3
▪

"Time-Out"

A little three-year-old was driving with her father. A man ran a yellow light and barely missed them. The daddy screamed, "You stupid son of a ——." The little girl looked at her father. "Oh, Daddy, shame on you. *Stupid*'s a bad word. You better go on 'Time-Out'."

THE BIG "TIME-OUT"

"Time-Out" is a disciplinary technique for use with children ages two through ten. "Time-Out" is a simple and very effective form of "corrective feedback." Your child is told that his or her behavior is inappropriate and is given a chance to behave correctly. If the inappropriate behavior continues, then the parent **calmly** tells the child that she is going to "Time-Out." Your child is then put in a boring place for a few minutes—typically a chair facing the corner of a room or hallway. When your child has finished her "Time-Out," she has paid her dues, and all is now forgiven. This is important. Don't keep chastising your child after "Time-Out" is over.

"Time-Out" has several advantages over traditional disciplinary approaches. First, your child's behavior is clearly labeled as inappropriate so that she knows what she is being corrected for. Your child is given a chance to comply (usually within five to ten seconds), but if this doesn't happen, she is put into a situation that clearly indicates that she did something wrong. Second, because "Time-Out" does not involve yelling or hitting, there is little chance that the situation will escalate if the parent uses the technique appropriately. Finally, "Time-Out" gives both the parent and the child the opportunity to calm down and start over.

The following three tables describe in detail how to use "Time-Out" correctly and what to do if it does not work successfully at first. By carefully following the techniques presented in these three tables, the vast majority of parents will be successful in decreasing the common behavior problems of young children.

Finally, for "Time-Out" to be an effective socialization technique, **it must be used frequently**. If you view "Time-Out" as a socialization method, then it makes intuitive sense to use it many times during the day (particularly with toddlers) as an essential part of teaching your child the rules and regulations (expectations) of our society. Also, it is important to use "Time-Out" **early**, before your child's behavior escalates in intensity or you become more and more emotionally upset. If you find yourself becoming angry, that means you let your child's behavior go too far. "Time-Out" is most effective when you can implement it **calmly** and **often**. If you become upset, use that as a cue or red light that **you made a mistake** by letting your child's behavior escalate to the point where you became frustrated and mad at your child. Also, **never** give a command that you do not intend to back up with consequences. Try not to repeat a command more than once.

It is essential not to wait **too long** to use "Time-Out." Parents are often reluctant to immediately put their child in "Time-Out." They wait and wait, **hoping** their child will listen. But young children aren't great listeners, and the only way to teach the process of good listening is by using "Time-Out" every time your child's behavior is inappropriate. We cannot emphasize this enough. A child does not have to drown the dog or knock her brother's teeth out for you to use "Time-Out."

Not listening, whining constantly, and refusing to take a bath are good enough reasons to use "Time-Out." Don't think of "Time-Out" as this horrible punishment. That will stop you from using it.
Try not to yell at your child. Often, when we are angry, we snap at our children. Some parents will ask their child to do something as if asking for a favor. This is **not** recommended. Make your request simple and direct. Wait about five to ten seconds. If

your child does not comply, tell her that she will get a "Time-Out." Then, wait another five to ten seconds. If your child doesn't listen, it's "Time-Out." It is essential to remember that if you threaten to use "Time-Out" several times before actually using it, you are teaching your child to ignore your first four or five commands because she knows you are not going to follow through initially. This will only make you angry and frustrated, and you will probably end up yelling at your child. Thus, don't threaten, do it!

"TIME-OUT" AS SOCIALIZATION

Kids are social animals. Peer acceptance is vitally important to young children. Toddlers are especially curious about children their age. They like to play with, touch, and explore one another. Even more important for children is parental approval. But toddlers will test everyone who crosses their paths. They want to see how far they can push until someone says, "Stop!" In a way, limit testing is a child's way of socializing. They are finding out where their boundaries are. But be assured, children want limits. They need limits. Otherwise, their world appears to be chaotic and disordered. Children feel more secure when they are loved **and** disciplined consistently and without yelling, screaming, or hitting.

Socialization is the first step in helping children learn the rules and behaviors acceptable to society. A large part of early socialization occurs when parents reward and discipline their child's behaviors. Thus, early in life children are gradually taught by their parents' feedback what is right and wrong behavior. You can help your child achieve positive relationships with peers by successfully handling her behavior problems, thereby teaching her socially acceptable rules.

The principle behind "Time-Out" is called "social learning theory," which asserts that children learn most of their behavior by observing others (particularly their parents) and by the consequences that follow their behaviors.

Thus, if you yell at or hit your child when he misbehaves, then you are teaching your child that you handle conflict by hitting and yelling. It is certainly guaranteed that you will be the recipient of your child's yelling, and possibly hitting, as your child grows older and you experience disagreements and conflicts. It's the "you get what you give out" theory. By using "Time-Out" you are teaching your child an important lesson about how to handle conflict, that is, to **stop and think** about the situation first. When your toddler is in "Time-Out," she has the opportunity to gradually calm down and to think about what she did that resulted in her being placed in "Time-Out." In contrast, **if you yell at your child, she will react to your yelling, rather than thinking about why she is in "Time-Out."**

"Time-Out" is also a subtle but highly effective way of teaching self-control. Whenever your child goes into "Time-Out" without having to be dragged or led there and then stays there for the full time without getting up or screaming for the duration, she is showing a tremendous amount of self-regulation of her behavior—that is, self-control. This process of self-regulation of behavior then begins to generalize to other situations that demand self-control, and teaching good self-control is part of socializing your child for interactions with others.

It is important to realize that children acquire traits like eye and hair color as well as certain personality traits through genetics. Therefore, try to assess your personality and your spouse's in order to realize that a temperamentally difficult child may be a genetic reflection of her parents or grandparents. Knowing this can relieve some of the guilt if you feel you are failing as a parent when your child constantly battles you. You'll just have to stay with it. If you are consistent and persistent in your use of "Time-Out," even a temperamentally difficult child will eventually come around.

Once you clearly understand the effect of your actions on your child's behavior, then the stage is set for "Time-Out" to work. Disciplining your child is the most difficult and important aspect of parenting. **How** you discipline your child (for example, hitting, yelling, or "Time-Out") can have a profound effect on your child's long-term emotional adjustment. By **using "Time-Out" often** and **without yelling or hitting**, you will be teaching your child the rules of the household and helping her learn to adapt to society's rules as well without causing emotional distress.

One Parent's Experience

Before the "Time-Out" era came to be, Susan was a spanker and a yeller. This led to her daughter's rage and the beginning of hurting her self-worth. It lasted only a few months. Susan was lucky enough to find the announcement for the parent's group. She now feels that creating positive self-esteem through disciplining with "Time-Out" is the single most important thing she could give her child.

"When I see her put her dolls on 'Time-Out,' explain to them what they did wrong, and then kiss them after 'Time-Out,' " explained Susan, "I know she feels good about herself. It is certainly better than seeing Barbie get flung against the wall and watching her head roll off."

Spanking, although advocated by some child experts, felt abusive for Susan and her husband, Alan. "I'm not talking about one light spank on the behind when a child refuses to stay in the 'Time-Out' chair. I mean constant spankings as the only form of discipline in the home. It is an angry, and in some ways a destructive act," she says.

Susan couldn't stand herself after she had spanked her daughter. "I was seriously shaken up with guilt and remorse." "Time-Out" is not violent and definitely a more loving approach. It is also a method commonly used in school situations, so it can be carried out at home with the same consistency.

"Time-Out" Steps

1. Buy a kitchen timer or any timer that "dings."

2. Designate a corner for the "Time-Out" chair; preferably in a boring hallway or room that you can easily monitor. Do not use your child's bedroom for "Time-Out."

3. Be sure to practice "Time-Out" steps with your child first before you begin to use it.

4. Choose a "Time-Out" chair; that is, tell your child that when she does something wrong, she will have to sit on the "Time-Out" chair until the timer goes off.

5. When your child misbehaves, tell her exactly what she did wrong (for example, "You didn't pick up your toys when I asked you to").

6. Tell your child to go to the "Time-Out" chair, and help her if needed (for instance, gently grasp her wrist firmly and lead her there).

7. Set the timer for one minute for each year of your child's age (for example, three minutes for three-year-olds).

8. Initially, your child has to be quiet for at least 30 seconds before the timer goes off, otherwise, reset the timer.

9. After your child has had several days of being quiet at least 30 seconds before the timer goes off, gradually increase the quiet time by 30-second intervals until she has to be quiet the whole time. Thereafter, reset the timer when she acts out in the "Time-Out" chair at any time, not just at the end.

10. If your child gets off the "Time-Out" chair before the timer goes off, give her *one* swat on the rear end and lead her back to the "Time-Out" chair *without* saying a word.

HOW TO USE "TIME-OUT" SUCCESSFULLY—"PRACTICE PLAYS"

1. Before using "Time-Out," practice using it with your child.
2. Tell your child that there are several rules when in "Time-Out":
   a. The timer will be set when she is quiet.
   b. If she leaves the chair before the timer goes off, you will give her **one** swat on the bottom and place her back in the chair.
3. Tell your child you will be using the "Time-Out" chair instead of yelling, threatening, or hitting. **Remind** yourself of this rule—**often**.
4. To increase the effectiveness of "Time-Out," be certain to "catch 'em being good" **often**. A child will act out to get her parents' attention. It is better than being ignored completely.
5. Ignore statements by your child that "Time-Out" doesn't bother her. It is simply a manipulative attempt to get you to not use "Time-Out."
6. When you first begin using "Time-Out," your child may act like "Time-Out" is a game. She may put herself in "Time-Out" or ask to go there. If this happens, play the game. That is, put her in "Time-Out" and require her to sit quietly for the required amount of time. She will soon learn that "Time-Out" is not fun. Your child may also laugh or giggle when being placed in "Time-Out" or while in "Time-

Out." Although this may aggravate you, it is important for you to **ignore** her completely when she is in "Time-Out."

7. You may feel the need to punish your child for doing something inappropriate in the chair (for example, cursing or spitting). It is, however, very important to ignore your child when she behaves badly in "Time-Out." This will teach her that such attention-getting strategies will **not** work. If your child curses when out of the chair (and it bothers you), be sure to put her in "Time-Out," even if it is a minute after she has left the chair.

8. Television, radio, or other children can make "Time-Out" more tolerable and prolong the length of time your child must stay in the chair by encouraging her to talk. Make sure there are no distractions. A nice, blank wall to look at is perfect.

9. Make sure that your child is aware of the house rules and that if they are broken, it will result in "Time-Out." Frequently, parents will establish a new rule ("Don't climb on the new couch") without telling their children. When children unwittingly break the new rule, they don't understand why they are being put in "Time-Out."

10. Your child may not leave the chair to go to the bathroom, get a drink, or get her security blanket. If a child goes to "Time-Out" during

a meal, she should miss that portion of the meal. Do not make extra fun snacks to compensate for the missed meal.

11. When your child is in "Time-Out," think of her as being in a spaceship in outerspace and totally **inaccessible** to you.

12. Remember to reset the timer when your child acts out when in "Time-Out." This teaches your child that she has to stop and think before you will let her finish her "Time-Out."

What If Your Child Refuses to Go to the "Time-Out" Chair?

If your child delays or refuses to go to the "Time-Out" chair, gently grasp her wrist firmly and lead her there without saying a word. Very young children can be picked up and placed in "Time-Out." Alternatively, for an older child, tell her that if she does not go to the chair immediately, you will add an additional minute for each ten seconds that she delays. If after adding two additional minutes your child continues to refuse to go to the chair, then remove all privileges until she spends the full amount of time (plus penalty time) in the chair. For example, your child loses all television time, toys, computer games, radio, telephones, playing outside, and so on for the day until she spends her time in the "Time-Out" chair.

What If Your Child Leaves the Chair Without Permission?

Many children will test their parents' authority when "Time-Out" is first used. They will try to escape from the chair before time is up. Your child should be warned about this during the first practice "Time-Out." If your child leaves "Time-Out," the following should be done:

1. The first time your child leaves the chair, put her back in the chair and say, loudly and with a stern appearance, "If you get out of that chair again, I am going to spank you!" (Clap your hands loudly in front of your child when you say the word *spank*.)

2. When your child leaves the chair again, **one** swift swat across the **buttocks** is all that is needed. **Do not** take the child's pants down to do this. YOU ARE NOT TO HIT YOUR CHILD WITH ANY OBJECT OTHER THAN YOUR OPEN HAND!!! Return your child to the chair without saying a word.

3. Thereafter your child is to be spanked **once** each time that she leaves the chair. This is true even if your child is sent to "Time-Out" again for some other misbehavior. If your child leaves the chair without permission, **do not** give the warning again, but go straight to the one spank on the bottom described above.

The spanking procedure has been shown to be quite effective, and the vast majority of children require less than two or three spankings **total** before learning to stay on the chair when told to go there. Many do not even need one spanking, provided the warning described above is given properly.

If spanking is used, it should be used only for leaving the chair without permission, not for any other form of misbehavior. **Spanking should be used only for backing up "Time-Out," not as a primary discipline technique for misbehavior.**

If as a parent you object to spanking, even to back up the "Time-Out" chair procedure, a few alternatives exist. Unfortunately they take a longer period of time to be effective in keeping your child seated during "Time-Out." These alternatives are:

1. Each time your child gets out of the "Time-Out" chair, return her to the chair without a word and reset the timer; or

2. Kneel down behind the chair and grasp each of your child's wrists. Hold your child's arms at his side until there is clearly no resistance. Gradually release your grasp and stand up. If your child stays in the chair, then walk away without a word and reset the timer. If your child begins to get up, kneel down again and repeat the above procedure. This can take awhile, so be prepared to set aside whatever amount of time is needed; or

3. Each time your child gets up from the chair, return her to it and tell her that every time she gets up you will reset the timer. If she continues to get up after repeating this procedure

twice, then tell her that she loses all privileges for the day until she stays in "Time-Out" (for instance, say, "No television until you finish your 'Time-Out' "). Don't discuss this further with your child. Simply make the statement of the privilege-removal contingency, and then walk away. Be certain to follow through on the removal of the privileges.

Clearly, one spank on the bottom works more effectively. But, if your child continues to refuse to stay in the "Time-Out" chair after you've tried all alternatives, then it is time to seek professional help.

What to Expect the First Week

If your child follows the pattern typical of most children, you can expect that she will become quite upset when first sent to "Time-Out." Children may become quite angry and vocal while in "Time-Out" or may cry because their feelings have been hurt. They may call you names and even scream. It is important not to respond and not to look at them. This prolonged tantrum or crying will result in many children remaining in "Time-Out" well past their minimum time because they are not yet quiet. They may, therefore, spend anywhere from 30 minutes to an hour during the first "Time-Out" before becoming quiet and agreeing to do what was asked of them. Although this can seem excessive at first, it will work if you do not get deterred. It is not uncommon for **temperamentally difficult children** to fight you during the first week you use "Time-Out." **If this does not decrease by day four and five, then it is time to seek professional help.** With each use of "Time-Out" after that, you will find that your child becomes quiet much sooner. Eventually, your child will be quiet for most or all of the minimum time and will agree to do what was asked immediately thereafter. You will also find that your child will begin to obey your first commands, so that the frequency of "Time-Out" eventually decreases. This, however, may take several weeks to achieve. Try to remember during this first week of "Time-Out" that you are not harming your child, but helping to teach her better self-control, respect for parental authority, and the ability to follow rules. Your child may not like this method, but discipline is necessary if children are to learn what is expected of them within their families and society. If the end result is that you don't yell at your child anymore, your child will be happier in the long term.

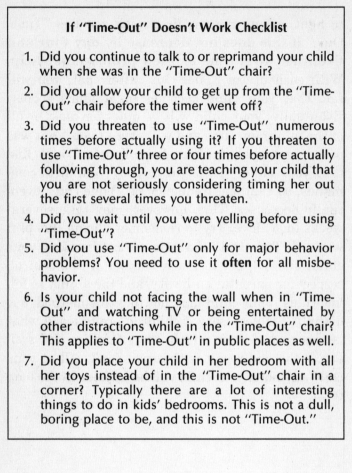

If "Time-Out" Doesn't Work Checklist

1. Did you continue to talk to or reprimand your child when she was in the "Time-Out" chair?

2. Did you allow your child to get up from the "Time-Out" chair before the timer went off?

3. Did you threaten to use "Time-Out" numerous times before actually using it? If you threaten to use "Time-Out" three or four times before actually following through, you are teaching your child that you are not seriously considering timing her out the first several times you threaten.

4. Did you wait until you were yelling before using "Time-Out"?

5. Did you use "Time-Out" only for major behavior problems? You need to use it **often** for all misbehavior.

6. Is your child not facing the wall when in "Time-Out" and watching TV or being entertained by other distractions while in the "Time-Out" chair? This applies to "Time-Out" in public places as well.

7. Did you place your child in her bedroom with all her toys instead of in the "Time-Out" chair in a corner? Typically there are a lot of interesting things to do in kids' bedrooms. This is not a dull, boring place to be, and this is not "Time-Out."

"Time-Out" Problem-Solving Checklist

1. Use your anger as a cue. That is, if you allow your child's behavior to escalate to the point where you get emotionally upset, then you didn't catch your child's behavior problem early enough.

2. Your husband/wife (grandparent, baby-sitter) undermines "Time-Out" by not using it themselves; by not supporting you for using it; and/or by disagreeing with you in front of your child on matters of discipline.

3. Be certain to use "Time-Out" with all your children.

4. You forget that "Time-Out" is an "instructional" technique—that is, it is a way of teaching your child what you expect in terms of socially appropriate behavior. Thus, **you need to use it a lot, the more the better, so that your child can learn what is expected of her**. Even minor behavior problems need "Time-Out."

5. Remember, "Time-Out" is simply corrective feedback. It is not some horrible punishment. It is **not** yelling, screaming, or hitting your child. It is an opportunity for your child to **stop and think** about what she did wrong.

6. It is essential to use "Time-Out" in combination with a lot of praise and positive attention for your child's appropriate behavior. Always remember the phrase, **"Catch 'em being good!"**

Bedside Checklist

Although you may be tempted to respond when your child is crying hysterically in "Time Out," it is **vital** to follow these points:

1. Do not talk to your child.
2. Do not even glance at her.
3. Do not talk with your spouse or anyone else about her if she can hear you.
4. **Try** not to show anger.
5. If possible, keep your composure.
6. Reread the "Time-Out" steps in the book.
7. Occupy yourself with another activity while monitoring your child.

4

Behavior in Public Places

Taking a toddler out to any place other than Mc-Donald's or Chuck E. Cheese can be a challenging experience. Shopping trips to elegant department stores, where you will be passing counters filled with Lalique and Baccarat is not advised. Also, shopping trips to Saks, where sticky fingers could land on an Yves Saint Laurent original, is not a good idea either. Save those excursions for yourself. Serious shopping takes serious thought, and while you are concentrating on your purchase, your little tot could wander off on an excursion of her own.

To encourage good behavior in public places, it is best to give your toddler a fighting chance in the beginning. Take her to the grocery store, a toy store, or someplace you can give her complete attention and encourage appropriate behavior. Think of these times as training trips. Try to make your trips as fun and educational as you can.

No situation is perfect, but **try** to follow the outlined suggestions as closely as possible:

TRAINING TIPS

1. Your first trips should not exceed a half hour and could be as little as ten minutes for younger children. (Maybe just go to buy a newspaper or to get milk.)

2. Choose a time when the store or restaurant is not very busy.

3. First outings should be for teaching, not for shopping or eating.

4. Rules should be explained **prior** to leaving the house or apartment as matter-of-factly as possible and restated immediately **prior** to entering the "training area." Some suggestions for rules include:
   a. Stay with Mom or Dad. Do not walk away alone.
   b. Do not pick up, touch, or play with things without permission from Mom or Dad.
   c. I will not buy you anything on this trip.

5. Provide your child with a lot of nonverbal, physical contact (at least once every minute or half minute) for appropriate behaviors. Occasionally offer verbal praise, such as, "Jake, you sure are being good," "You're staying right next to Mommy," "Thank you for not picking up any candy," or "It's easier to shop when you don't pick up things," "We'll do this again soon!"

6. Stay physically close to your child. Touch her gently on the back, give hugs, pulling her up next to you.

Now that you have all the dos, you probably are wondering if we've set you adrift in "public place purgatory." What if you try all of the rules and they all fail? Because we are all human (toddlers, too) and unpredictable beings, your child may not comply. The following suggestions will put you back on track.

"TIME-OUT" IN PUBLIC PLACES

The last time Karen put her daughter, Melissa, in "Time-Out" in Music Plus, Melissa started screaming at the top of her lungs. Two saleswomen came over and stared at Karen, shaking their heads. Her husband quickly left the immediate area as Karen broke out in a sweat.

Although discipline in public places can be difficult, it is vitally important to follow through with "Time-Out" when you are outside your home. Some of the following examples will help you find an appropriate place for "Time-Out" when you are not at home.

Remember to **follow through** no matter how many dirty looks you get. If you don't you may never want to take your child out with you, and this would be unfair to both of you. People with children will totally understand, and people without children will find out one day. It's better to have a few days of misery than many miserable years of incorrigible behavior.

In Department Stores

Take your child to an uncrowded aisle that is not used a lot by others and place your child facing a dull side of a display counter or a boring corner. If possible, it is more desirable to use the gift wrap or credit department area, rest room, or a changing or dressing room if nearby. Use a maternity section or kid's department. (It is not very busy, and there are sympathetic moms there!)

In Grocery Stores

Have your child face the side of a frozen foods counter (avoid the urge to put your child in the counter itself!); take your child to the farthest corner of the store; find the greeting card display and have your child face the walled side of the counter while you look at cards. Most grocery stores are difficult for finding a boring "Time-Out" place, so you may have to use one of the alternatives to "Time-Out" listed below.

In a Place of Worship

Take your child to the kid's room where mothers take crying babies during the service; use the foyer or entryway; use a rest room off the lobby.

In a Restaurant

Turn your child's chair away from the table. If this is not enough to control her behavior, then use the rest rooms or an empty booth as the "Time-Out" site or go outside.

At a Friend's House

Be sure to explain to your friend that you are using a new behavioral method and you may need to place your child in a chair or stand your child in a corner or hallway if he misbehaves. Ask you friend where one could be used.

During a Long Car Trip

Review the rules with your child and set up your expectations before having your child enter the car. Be sure to take along games or activities for your child to do during the trip as well as juice boxes and snacks. If you need to discipline your child, pull off the road to a safe stopping area and have your child serve the "Time-Out" on the floor of the backseat. **Never leave your child in the car unattended.**

If you use "Time-Out" in a public place, it may take only half the normal time because "Time-Out" in public places is very effective with children. Also, if your child leaves "Time-Out" without permission, use the same procedure you have been using at home for this (usually one swift spank to the buttocks is needed in such cases). **Be strong.**

IF YOU CANNOT USE "TIME-OUT" IN THE PUBLIC PLACE

There are always a few places where putting your child in a corner for misbehavior is just not possible. Here are some alternatives, but they should be used ONLY WHERE YOU CANNOT FIND A "TIME-OUT" AREA:

1. Take your child outside of the building and have her face the wall.

2. Take your child back to your car and have her sit on the floor of the backseat. Stay in the front seat or beside the car.

3. Take along a small spiral notepad. Before entering the public place, tell your child that you will write down any episode of misbehavior and that he will have to go to "Time-Out" as soon as you get home. Add an extra minute to "Time-Out" for each misbehavior after the first one.

Remember, do not leave your child unattended when he is in "Time-Out." Stay close by and turn your back. **Do not talk** to him. Also make sure to act quickly, so it does not escalate to a loud confrontation or temper tantrum. Finally, it is also important to remember that using "Time-Out" in public places has a much higher chance of working effectively if you **first** establish "Time-Out" successfully for behavior problems at home.

5
—————— ▪ ——————

Mom and Dad Support System

—————— ▪ ——————

PARENT POWER

Perhaps the single most important point in our book is that **parents' behavior is a major determinant of their children's behavior**. The use of "Time-Out" alone will not only vary from parent to parent, but the success of "Time-Out" depends on the parents' awareness of their own behavior and how they react to their children's behavior.

Barbara and her daughter, Brittany, took a trip with her friend, Shirley, and her four-year-old daughter to Colorado. Shirley and Barbara are both avid "Time-Out" users. What was so interesting was their different methods of using "Time-Out" and how it affected them emotionally. Shirley used "Time-Out" regularly and with a great deal of calm in her voice and demeanor. She was by nature a more patient and "work it through" sort of person than Barbara. Yet, she admitted that she was a wreck inside. Barbara, on the other hand, was quick-tempered and easily fell prey to emotional hysteria when her daughter pushed her too far. By the time Barbara used "Time-Out," she was **very** angry, and her emotions were more external.

"Time-Out" became an emotional control for Shirley. For Barbara, it became an emotional up-heaval. Barbara decided to explore this issue. What she discovered seemed profound. Children are bright, intuitive, emotional beings who soak up and **imitate their parents' behavior**. Barbara's daughter at barely four years old discovered that by with-drawing her affection from her mother, she held a great deal of power. As Brittany withdrew, Barbara became less involved in the process of discipline in the hopes of winning back Brittany's hugs and kisses. This lesson was extremely painful. As mature as Barbara liked to believe she was, she actually sat down and cried when Brittany pushed her away and said she didn't want her.

Barbara had subconsciously transferred her parental power to her child. Brittany, who really didn't want it but certainly was using it, became more and more out of control. Then, if Barbara did put her in "Time-Out," Brittany would be especially rejecting afterward.

Her friend, Shirley, suggested she make light of the situation. If Brittany didn't want her, Shirley told Barbara to say, "OK, Mommy is over here if you need me." Barbara had to take a deep breath when she was angry and put Brittany in "Time-

Out" as calmly as she could. She made herself available if Brittany needed her but no longer **asked** for her affection.

In her mind Barbara worked through the concept that:

1. Brittany was her responsibility. She had to discipline and teach her in an appropriate way.

2. Brittany did not "owe" her affection and love.

3. Discipline gave her daughter a sense of security.

4. Parents cannot dump their emotional baggage on their child.

5. Every family has interactive dynamics that should be carefully explored.

The last issue is perhaps the most important. To set a disciplinary "ideal" will only lead parents toward frustration. In reality, different personalities respond to situations with varied emotional reactions. Not every parent will put their child in "Time-Out" for the same reasons. People's tolerance levels differ. The key is to try to create a norm that will establish boundaries with your child. Although Barbara was high-strung and quick-tempered, she learned to **stop and think** before she put her daughter in "Time-Out," to take a deep breath, and to calm down. Her child had learned to "push her buttons," and Barbara had to learn not to overreact.

MODELING—"YOU GET WHAT YOU GIVE OUT"

At eighteen months Allison would toddle around imitating her mother's actions. She would play with pots and pans, pretending to cook like Mommy. At two, Allison imitated Mommy when she put on her makeup, surveying herself in the mirror, carefully pretending to put on lipstick and rouge. At five, Allison saw Mommy and Daddy constantly shouting at each other. In turn, Allison started shouting and talking back to her friends, imitating her parents' actions. Her mother was concerned when the teacher wrote a note home telling her about Allison's behavior. Her mother didn't understand why her daughter was acting this way. "What had she done wrong?" Allison had never seemed like an aggressive child, and in truth, Allison wasn't an aggressive personality. She was imitating behavior she saw at home, and to Allison, this seemed appropriate.

Children learn through observation, particularly by observing their parents' interaction. Parents don't always see themselves as role models for children, but in reality, they are probably the **most** important role models a child will ever have. This responsibility is a great one, because it can set the stage for the child's behavior throughout his life. Children observe **everything**, so everything you do will have an impact. Observational learning is **the** major way that children learn about the complex social interactions of their world.

If you complain that your child watches too much television, it might be a good idea to monitor your own TV watching. If you tell your child not to eat late at night, and then he catches you snacking on cookies at bedtime, how is he supposed to react? Parents often set up double standards with their children, sometimes consciously, but usually they are not aware that they are doing so.

Children do learn by example, so it might serve you well to think about what strong lessons you want your child to get. This refers to values as well. If you are thoughtful of others, then chances are your children will be as well. If you are rude, then your children will probably tend to be rude.

The White Lie

Parents will tell children that it is OK to tell white lies (little lies that don't hurt anyone) to avoid uncomfortable social situations. By condoning this behavior, you are telling your child that he can lie, but at some point he will not always be able to distinguish between little white lies and big lies. It is very important with young children to emphasize telling the truth at all times. As they get older, they will learn the subtle social skills needed to avoid hurting someone's feelings by an unnecessary comment.

"I'm Sick" Routine

We can turn our kids into hypochondriacs by our behavior. How often do you complain about being tired, sick, bored? Your back hurts. Your head hurts. You're overweight. Your skin is sallow. You're overstressed. This type of modeling is socially destructive. Children can actually become depressed and anxious by constantly listening to complaints and modeling negative talk. Try to set a positive model by saying **positive** statements. For instance, "I had a stressful day, but I'm going to try and make it better!" "I don't want to be sick." But if a child does try to get your attention by feigning illnesses and you've determined he isn't ill, then ignore the behavior and reinforce your child when he is acting healthy again. You might say, "When you are healthy, there are so many fun activities we can do together."

Many overweight parents have overweight children, not so much because of what they feed them, but because of what they say. If a parent obsesses over food and has a food disorder, then it is very likely that the child will eventually develop inappropriate eating habits. Your eating behavior will have an effect on how your child eats. Do not force your child to clean his plate. It may produce eating beyond satiety.

We started the chapter by telling you how important it is to understand your family dynamics. There are **no** perfect parents or children. But hopefully there are parents who are more mature than their small children. That means, if you spend time discussing and thinking through how your behavior might adversely affect your child's, it will be worth the effort.

It is also just as important to explore the wife–husband dynamics. How we treat one another is just as valuable in teaching our children appropriate and inappropriate interaction with others. Yet we don't advocate unrealistic change.

You can't pretend problems don't exist if they do. Stress and life's vicissitudes are part of marriage and being human. Children can't be totally sheltered in a world of false emotion. But as much as possible, we should try to regard one another with respect and honesty.

One mother in the parent's group was emotionally moved by her five-year-old when the boy apologized to her (after "Time-Out") in the same manner her husband had apologized that same morning over an incident between them. Children learn by observing—even when we may not be aware they are even watching us!

It's important for parents to show affection, to apologize to one another, to give family hugs, to tell children that it is OK for Mommy and Daddy to be angry with each other, and to say I love you to their children and each other. The following guidelines further support the premise that the way parents interact between themselves and with their child can profoundly affect the success or failure of using the recommended discipline techniques.

GUIDELINES FOR SUCCESSFUL PARENTAL DISCIPLINE—RED LIGHTS

Red lights are internal signals or cues that go off when we know something isn't right. Most red lights are caused because we have unrealistic expectations of our children. Children younger than six **cannot reason abstractly**. They don't have the ability to grasp long, verbal explanations by their parents. Children's inability to deal with abstractions will only frustrate them and their parents if parents try to use logic with toddlers.

Parents may have a seemingly stimulating conversation with their child. They may give the child directions, and the child may even respond. All this terrific interaction may appear to be ideal until the child does the opposite of what is expected. It is important to remember that just because children's verbal behavior makes them sound like little adults, the reality is that cognitively they have not yet reached a level of understanding that allows them to truly master abstract reasoning or to use logical thought.

Sometimes when a child does something he knows he's not allowed to do, parents don't realize that the child is not able to fully comprehend this. Telling a child something repeatedly and then assuming he knows it, is a red light.

Red Light—Assumptions

If you assume your child understands something, you will be frustrated when he or she doesn't listen.

To your child your conversations with him will seem negative, and he'll get the message that you are angry.

Red Light—Encouraging Misbehavior by Being Inattentive

Have you ever been in parent heaven when you discover your toddler playing quietly? One mother found herself on her hands and knees crawling past her three-year-old daughter's door so as not to disturb her. Hard as this is to believe, when you actively try to avoid making contact with your child, you are ignoring him.

Your child will eventually pick up on your tactics. Children know that if they want Mommy or Daddy's attention, all they have to do is cause trouble and their parents will come running. If you use "Time-Out" consistently and do not ignore your child when he is playing quietly, but rather **reinforce** (as we've said many times before) their good behavior, your child will get the message that "he can get lots of attention by **not** misbehaving."

Red Light—Missed Signals

"You say yes, he says no." If parents give different signals to a child, that child will be confused and frustrated. Clarify the rules of the house and have **all** family members stick to them. The inconsistency can also lead your child to use manipulative behavior, because he will see that Mom and Dad are not a cohesive unit. If Dad says no, he may go to Mom and begin playing one off the other. Even in a divorce situation, it is important to remain a parent team.

Red Light—Threatening and Not Following Through

This is a big one. When you say to Johnny ten times, "If you shake the goldfish bowl one more time, I'll . . ." and you don't follow through after one threat, then Johnny will catch on that you are not serious. In fact, to some children this becomes a game and a challenge. It's called "Let's see how crazy one can make Mom and Dad until they scream."

If you do put your child in "Time-Out" after three to four threats, then its full effectiveness is lost because your child already knows that the first three to four threats don't count. So actually, you've taught your child not to listen the first three to four times. Use no more than one threat, and then follow with "Time-Out" if your child is still noncompliant.

Points to Remember Checklist

1. Don't **argue** about how you should discipline your child in front of her. This will divide you and your spouse, and your child will eventually learn how to play one parent against the other.
2. Never give a command or request if you don't intend to **enforce** it.
3. Discuss what behavior you both consider appropriate or inappropriate.
4. **Both** of you should explain to your child what discipline will occur if he misbehaves. Be specific.
5. You and your spouse should be **consistent**. Use the same discipline or reward all the time for the same behaviors.
6. If your child whines and protests, restate your position and walk away.
7. If one of you is disciplining your child, and the other walks in, the other should not interfere with the discipline—even if he or she disagrees with the procedure. Discuss disagreements later behind closed doors.
8. SHARE—that means good and bad. Take **equal** responsibility for discipline.

MOMMY, I HATE YOU

The first time your child says, "I hate you," the knife will pierce your heart. You may get angry, you may even cry. Whatever you do, you'll definitely be shocked that this child, whom you love more than life itself, could say such words to you.

But children don't really hate us. They are simply trying to establish a sense of control and independence. It's their way of saying, "Let me be me. Let me be free." It's the parents' responsibility to recognize that while the child's attempts to "do it on their own" is normal, they don't have the cognitive abilities yet to make the proper choices. This is where "Time-Out" begins to educate the child, through a constructive daily learning process of corrective feedback and positive reinforcement, about the right and wrong choices.

Young children, like teenagers, are struggling for independence! When you set rules and discipline, they feel stifled. But love and hate are intense emotions that are closely related. If you let children be themselves, give them room, but set limitations, they'll feel safe and they'll be thankful for your love, even if they don't shower you with hugs and kisses.

It's also important that children understand that you have moods and feelings as well. Some days you may be short-tempered, feeling ill, or distracted. You may not be a perfect parent every day, and that's **okay**! Let your child know, without giving too much detail, that you are upset or tired or ill. You may not always get the child's understanding, because toddlers are "me, me, I, I" beings. Eventually, though, your child will understand and will love you even more for having the loving honesty to say, "I'm sorry," and for being honest about your feelings. That's really all we can ask of one another—even of children.

SPOILING

Give me, get me, do for me, buy me, take me! The story of a spoiled child is taught, not born. Values are what we teach our children from a very early age. Most parents think spoiling is strictly related to material objects.

Yet spoiling has to do with how we respond to a child from toddlerhood. If every time you walk into a store, you buy your child a toy, if every time your child makes a demand, you jump to it on command, if you always put your child's desires before yours or others, then indeed he may be spoiled.

It's very difficult to say, "No," when two big, adorable eyes are begging for something. But a child knows no limits unless you establish them. We often tend to say no, and then give in. We think children are spoiled only if we give them too many things. Children who are spoiled often come from permissive and materialistic families. These are not necessarily wealthy families.

When we worry that our children will not get the best of everything, that they will be deprived, it is necessary to look to our own personal motivations. Our own feelings of deprivation may invade their world. Children may grow up unable to cope with life's simplest problems because they are so used to getting everything when they want it—immediate gratification. They become immature adults who expect Mommy and Daddy to fulfill their every need and bail them out of every unpleasant situation.

Part of helping a child become a caring adult is

building his sense of respect for other people. It all boils down to values. If parents act as positive role models, showing their children that it is important to give to others, then their children have a better chance of not being spoiled, of becoming empathetic adults.

Try to have a monthly activity. Give food or clothes to your favorite charity, work for the environment, make toys for needy children. Let your child **see** how good it **feels** to give and not just to get.

Part of dealing with the out-of-control, spoiled child has to do with consistent discipline. Try to use the same disciplinary approach (in this case "Time-Out") every time your child misbehaves. As we've mentioned before, **set limits** and **rules before** you leave the house. If your child whines, screams, or manipulates, asking you for toys and food, immediately put him in "Time-Out."

Once you have said, "No," do not back down unless you are willing to pay the consequences. Often parents give in, become angry at themselves, and then take it out on their child. Decide what your limits are before you take your child out. Establish those limits.

Another approach to use when your child is whining or begging for something is the point system. Some people use gold stars, others use work-chore charts (discussed in detail in Chapter 11), or as a child gets older, they can get an allowance. By the contingent reward method, children learn that they have a responsibility to complete a task before they earn privileges. This can help build their feelings of self-worth as well. Don't always think in terms of money or toy rewards. Sometimes just a hug or words of praise will be welcome rewards.

It is important to look at children's reactions to the things they do get. Some children are never satisfied, and if they are, it is often only temporary. They cannot seem to be satiated. If this is the case, it's important to look deeper. Perhaps the child is craving attention and needs **you** more than his toys. Perhaps, he has been given too much, and each new thing holds no excitement, no importance. Whatever the reason, pay attention to these signs.

One last important point to remember: When you do give, give freely. Attach no conditions if you decide to give your child a gift. All other rewards should be given contingent on appropriate behavior.

Giving should not be a reason for your child to like you, love you, respect you, or behave better. Like love, giving should be unconditional. If it is not, the gift becomes tainted. And this is the point where a child can feel deprived no matter how much he has sitting in his toybox. These feelings will carry over into adulthood. Parents have to earn the same love and respect that children do. Love cannot be bought with a new toy. Instead, spend more time with your child.

BABY BURNOUT

Baby burnout is like a work burnout—too much can leave you exhausted, depressed, nervous, and frazzled. You love your kids, and you may love your work, but too much interaction can stress out both the child and the parent.

Part of the problem with burnout is that we fail to recognize it before it is too late. By too late we mean, before you are screaming, being verbally abusive, or even hitting your child.

By this point, "Time-Out" may be useless. You're upset and your child is upset. Young children don't always understand when Mom or Dad says, "I need time alone." Even an undemanding child will need you to help him with a hundred different things, and, yes, this is your responsibility as a parent. But responsibility extends to your breaking point.

Your first responsibility is to determine how far you can go until you lose control. When you feel you can't handle your child, it's best to retreat.

- Leave the room.

- Ask a neighbor to come over.

- Ask your spouse to take over for you.

- Ask a caregiver to watch your child.

Of course, the perfect scenario (if possible)—and usually this is a big "if" with parents—is to take a short vacation. Sometimes even an overnight stay somewhere can be helpful.

Parents are often upset because they "lose it." They scream and yell and experience a part of themselves they never realized existed. The truth is, all of us have that negative side. Most people ask how to avoid losing their cool. As we've repeated before,

you must be willing to work in the beginning to get a lot in the end. It's worth the effort.

When one mother caught a glimpse of herself in the mirror while yelling at her three-year-old, she was frightened by the image of this crazed woman standing over this little toddler. She admitted she looked like the Wicked Witch of the West. At that point, she knew she was heading for burnout.

Six months later, after working consistently on "Time-Out," she felt like a different mother. She was much more in control of her emotions, and her relationship with her child improved.

6

Three Daily Dilemmas

MEALTIME, DRESSING, AND BEDTIME PROBLEMS

These seemingly natural things—dressing, sleeping, and eating—may not come so naturally to a young child. Young children quite frankly don't want to be bothered with such frivolities as manners, getting dressed quickly, and having to go to bed on time. Life up to this point has been one great narcissistic free-for-all. Babies dictate, and parents obey. When reasoning begins to emerge, so do limitations. Most children will push their limits for as long and as hard as they can. This new power surge both excites and frightens them. Every simple task like getting dressed or eating becomes a standoff situation.

It's really all right to indulge your toddler in some situations, especially if he is under two and a half, but by the time a child is four or five years old, he should be able to comply with your requests without an argument or hysterical outbursts.

Mealtime Behavior Problems

The quickest way to get a nervous stomach is to have problems with your toddler over meals. This seemingly natural thing, eating, is a big problem in families. Usually the parents worry that their child is not eating enough. Chances are, and most doctors will agree, that children will not starve to death—even if they are picky eaters. In fact, unlike most adults, children eat when they are hungry and, therefore, do not overstuff themselves unnecessarily.

In order to enjoy mealtimes, it is important to establish rules early on. Mealtimes are also when you will want to teach your child manners and the kind of behavior you will want him to exhibit outside of your home.

Like all other behaviors, the key once again is consistency. Establish reasonable rules for your child:

- Remain seated.

- Do not talk with food in your mouth.

- Do not leave the table until the meal is completed.

The individual rules will depend on you and the age of your child. But remember, it's important to always praise appropriate behavior, and do it often. Once you teach your rules and your child follows them, any infraction should be considered inappropriate.

The following guidelines will help get you on a course toward pleasant mealtimes rather than anxiety-filled, tension-fraught meals that end in yelling and Pepto-Bismol for dessert.

Talk to your child at mealtimes. Even if he is under two, you can still address him. If your child breaks a rule, that's "Time-Out."

1. Use "Time-Out" only twice during any one meal. If there is a third disruption, **the meal is over** for your child. That means, take away his plate regardless of how much has been eaten, and don't make a big production over this. Be matter-of-fact about it.

2. Do not allow your child to eat anything until the next meal.

3. If your child whines or persists, put him in "Time-Out."

4. Do not nag, threaten, or give warnings during mealtimes. After two or three instances mealtimes should be more enjoyable. Children **want your company**, and because meals are a good opportunity to be together, it is unlikely they will jeopardize your companionship, let alone their tummies.

Mealtimes are a good place to teach socially acceptable behavior. Some children get pleasure out of making you crazy by either not eating or taking two hours to complete a meal. Part of the problem comes from piling too much food on a child's plate. Put out small portions. It's better if they ask for seconds.

When your child eats, give encouragement. Don't send out the message, "Why aren't you eating your peas?" Instead say, "Look how great you use your fork," and, "You're sitting so quietly. How terrific!"

Hold out on dessert until the meal is finished. If he doesn't eat, then no dessert and no snacks. Parents overdo snacks. By the time a child has two or three snacks, they've eaten a meal. So they won't be hungry at mealtime. A snack after school should be limited to juice or milk and a small treat like raisins or fruit. Try to avoid giving sweets.

Attempt to hold out until meals. If your child is hungry, that's a good sign that he'll eat his meal. Don't think hunger means starvation.

For those children who like to dine and dine and dine, set the kitchen timer at a reasonable amount of time—around 30 minutes. When the timer rings, the meal is over. Your toddler may be a bit surprised at first, but this will help him to get in the habit of eating his meal within a certain amount of time.

Thirty minutes is **a lot** of time to eat. But if you feel uncomfortable, set the timer longer.

Remember, these are not rules cast in stone. Every child and every parent are different. We appreciate those differences. The guidelines we present are just that—guidelines. They've been used and proven to work. But feel free to adapt them to your life-style and your child's.

Dressing Behavior Problems

Dressing problems can leave a parent totally exhausted. You feel like you're ready to do battle.

A big mistake we all make is to let our kids watch television or start playing with their toys **before** they are dressed. Trying to pull a three-year-old away from a Ninja Turtles video is not an easy task.

Set up dressing rules:

- No TV before you are dressed.

- No toys before you are dressed.

- Give extra praise and give a small reward if your child can get himself dressed (if he's old enough).

- No food before you are dressed.

It's important to choose and set out his clothes the night before. It's not pleasant looking for one Mickey sock at 7 AM in a pile of 50 mismatched socks. Once you choose an outfit, unless the weather dictates otherwise, do not change it.

Let your child have some input. Unless it's a special occasion, let your child pick out his own pajamas, underwear, socks, and even two or three times a week, his own outfit. Don't laugh or tell them that they look funny. They probably will, but his self-esteem will be in great shape. Tell them what an interesting outfit they've chosen or how nice they look.

In order for your child's dressing routine to last no more than 20 to 30 minutes, which is reasonable, you should set the timer each day for a week or so. If your child is capable of dressing himself, check on him every five minutes. If he is not dressed when the timer rings, you should finish dressing him, but do not talk to your child except to give instructions.

If your child is dressed, **no matter how he looks**, praise him and even give a small reward (special playtime, treat after school or lunch, and so on).

If you cannot get your child to cooperate, immediately send him to "Time-Out." Do not nag him. Remember to follow a consistent routine.

Habits to Sleep By

A simple way to assure good sleep habits is to make sure your child is tired when he goes to sleep. Often the wrong foods, overstimulation, and lack of exercise during the day will inhibit a good night's sleep.

Exercise

Usually a child will exercise at school, but for preschoolers or those children in need of more exercise, make sure he gets playtime daily. This means long walks, a gym class, an hour or more at the park, and bike rides for older children.

Overstimulation

The goal is to try to calm and quiet your child before he goes to sleep. Also, try to help your young child put himself to sleep. Many children cannot get to sleep without a parent first reading to them, holding them, singing to them, or just sitting in the room. All of these activities are fine, but not if you **have to be** in the room for your child to fall asleep.

Although we've stressed how important exercise

is, do not let your child run and jump right before bedtime. Your toddler's adrenaline level will give him enough energy to stay up for hours! Turn off the television, read books, listen to soft music, or simply rub his back. Begin "quiet time" 30 minutes before bedtime.

Bedtime Behavior Problems

It's 10:00 PM. You and your husband have finally settled into bed. You start to cuddle. Suddenly a voice at your door says, "Mommy, I want some water." You get up and get your toddler some water. You return and start to cuddle up again. Then, the voice at your bedroom door returns. "Mommy, I have to go pee-pee." You jump out of bed. After a few minutes you are back. Just as you are about to climb in bed, "Mommy, there's a monster in my room." Your child runs into your bed. You get up, take your child into his room, and spend 15 minutes chasing away monsters. When you return to your spouse, he's fast asleep. Cuddles are over. Another night of bedtime blues.

Bedtime problems literally can become nightmares if they aren't stopped quickly. Besides your personal life disintegrating, you'll look awful. Some parents just forego sleeping, sex, and silence in order to pacify their child. But sleep problems can become chronic if not stopped and can cause emotional upheaval in a family.

The following suggestions should be used with children from the moment they can get out of their beds or cribs. As with "Time-Out," it is extremely important that you follow through. If you slip one night, you may have to start all over again.

1. Pick a reasonable bedtime (7 to 8:30 PM), or naptime, and under normal day-to-day circumstances put your child to bed at that time every time. Although you may want to allow a half-hour leeway on weekends, try to stay with the same bedtime until it becomes a habit.

2. About 30 minutes prior to bedtime, start "quiet time," during which your child should be occupied with quiet activities.

3. Set up a bedtime routine (bath, bedtime story, kisses, drinks, bathroom, and so on). If possible, stick to this routine even if you are on vacation.

4. Put your child in bed, tell him good night and that you will see him in the morning, turn off the light, leave the room, and close the door (optional). If your child likes a night-light, that is fine.

5. Watch your child **very closely** the first few nights, and catch him getting out of bed the instant he gets up.

6. When your child gets up, put him back in bed. Do not talk to him or act angry. Make this as matter-of-fact as possible. Do not tuck him in, soothe him, or even carry him in an affectionate manner.

7. Continue doing this each time he gets up. You

may be surprised how often he will get up the first few nights, but don't get discouraged—he is just testing to find out whether you really mean it. Don't give up.

8. In the morning, give lots of positive reinforcement to your child for staying in bed (if he did) and reward him with something like allowing him to choose between two different foods he likes. If he didn't stay in bed, say nothing.

Consistency is the key with bedtime problems. Some children may have a more serious sleep disorder. At some point, if you try everything with total follow-through and it doesn't work, we suggest you seek out a therapist who specializes in sleep-disorder problems.

With younger children (one to two years old) it is very important that they feel secure and safe when they go to sleep. Always have several stuffed animals and a blanket in his crib or bed that your child can use to comfort himself as he's learning to fall asleep alone. Not all children will take to a transitional object like a blanket, but if you provide one in the crib in infancy, there is a good chance that a child will eventually attach to the object. Most children will keep their "blankie" with them until they are around five or six or until it falls apart. This is normal. Never throw away a security blanket no matter how dirty or ratty it is.

There are numerous lullaby cassette tapes on the market, which can help lull your little one to sleep.

When you put on the tape, make sure the music is not too loud.

Crying is extremely distressing for parents. They worry that some horrible thing has happened to their child and find themselves running back and forth to their toddler's room every time they hear a peep. After a while, your child learns that the littlest cry will get them attention.

Here comes the hard part. If you don't want to get up and down all night, **do not** go into the room when your child cries; especially if this has become an established attention-getting pattern. He may cry for an hour or more. He may also make noises, yell, or call. DO NOT give in. The first time you break down your child will know what to do to get your attention. Don't get discouraged. This method should work after less than a week. Once your child is going to bed after crying for only a minute or two, you can go into the bedroom to check on him to make sure everything is all right.

For any bedtime crying, remember:

1. **Do not talk** to your child after he is down for the night.

2. Check his diapers (if applicable) quickly.

3. If everything is OK, leave the room quietly.

For children who have a habit of going into their parents' beds, the same rules apply:

1. Pick up your child and put him back in his bed as matter-of-factly as possible. Do this as many times as necessary, no matter how much he

protests. The first few times, you may have to do this ten times or more!

2. **Do not talk** to your child as you return him to his bed.

3. Be prepared to be **persistent**. One night in your bed is so reinforcing that it's almost guaranteed to become a regular habit.

4. After two to three nights (a week in long-standing cases), your child should begin to understand that sleeping in your bed is no longer acceptable behavior.

7

--- • ---

The Big Wa-Wa's

--- • ---

FAMILY FIT

As every mother knows who has more than one child, each child is fundamentally different from birth. From day one, some infants are fussy, cry a lot, don't sleep through the night, don't eat well, and in general are "difficult"; whereas the other child might do just the opposite, being the "easy" baby; meaning sleeping through the night, eating well, not fussing very much.

These personality traits, or child **temperament**, are part of behavioral genetics—that is, children acquire through genetics certain rather stable personality traits or temperament, much the same way that they acquire eye color, hair color, and other physical features inherited from their parents and their Uncle Harry.

While most children with "difficult temperaments" are very challenging to raise, a "good fit" between your child's temperament and the family environment can go a long way toward making family life more enjoyable. Conversely, a "poor fit" between your child's difficult temperament and your parenting style can result in constant battles and conflicts. "Time-Out" is a "good fit."

One child may be perceived as difficult by a parent, whereas the rest of the world perceives that child as easy. Some parents and children may have to accommodate one another when there is a "poor fit" temperamentally between them.

The best family environment for managing a child is using "Time-Out" without emotion. That is, without yelling or hitting.

Trish and her son, Jason, have a similar personality. They both have strong-willed stubborn temperaments. When Trish started to use "Time-Out," she would wait until she was too upset to use the technique properly. Trish seemed to be constantly angry with Jason, because his strong-willed behavior directly clashed with her own need to be in control. In order to resolve this type of conflict it is important to recognize that you **both** need "Time-Out" from the situation. Your anger will only set off your child's exaggerated emotional response to being timed out. When you feel that you are becoming uncontrollably angry, "Time-Out" your child and then "Time-Out" yourself by sitting down to stop and think about your overreaction. When you calm down, you can get up from your own personal "Time-Out."

* * *

Key Points

- Recognize that your child will react to your anger, and the conflict between the two of you will escalate.

- **Be neutral** when you use "Time-Out." You don't have to be pleasant, but you should have a businesslike demeanor. Be matter-of-fact.

SEPARATION ANXIETY

The first couple of times that you leave your child with a sitter or drop her off at a day-care center, it will probably be a very emotional experience for you. If you can treat these separations matter-of-factly, your child will learn to separate rather easily, making the whole process much less draining on both of you. Some additional suggestions follow:

1. Do not discuss the separation before it occurs. Doing so will not help, but it may make separating more difficult.

2. Plan ahead so that you can separate quickly. Have all of your child's things together in one bag or her toys out in one place so that you won't drag out the separation.

3. When it comes time to do so, separate as quickly and as matter-of-factly as possible.

4. If separating is hard for you, set up artificial opportunities to practice separating. For example, arrange to drop your child off at a friend or relative's house several additional

times each week until you become more proficient at it.

5. When you pick your child up, don't be overly emotional. It's OK to act glad to see her, but don't start crying and hugging her excessively—doing so only shows her how hard the separation was for you.

6. Generally the way children handle separation is a direct reflection of how their parents handle it. Do well and your child will do much better.

7. Realize that children who are temperamentally shy will always need gentle encouragement, nudging toward new or novel social situations. Once your child gets over the initial anxiety associated with the novel situation, she will be more willing to return to it in the future.

MANIPULATIVE BEHAVIOR

Manipulative behavior is most prevalent in the older toddler, ages three and a half to five. There are a number of kinds of manipulative behaviors, all with one goal—to get the child what she wants. Some children will use several methods simultaneously if they are having a tough time breaking down the parent. For example, some manipulative behaviors include asking for a hug in order to avoid "Time-Out," or trying to excuse the behavior by saying, "I won't do it again, Mommy."

To stop manipulative behavior be direct when

asking a child to do something. If you get into a push-pull argument with your child, you're in for trouble. Your child will find that her persistence is paying off by your increased attention—positive or negative.

It's important to pick your battles. If you try or insist on winning every battle, you'll be battling constantly. For small, inconsequential things, give in.

Remind your child that there are rules to follow and that the consequence for breaking the rules is "Time-Out." "Time-Out" should always be used with consistency.

Weekends are a good time to loosen up. If a child wants to stay up later, say, "On Friday or Saturday night, you can stay up fifteen minutes later." Also, let your child have one or two days where she can pick out whatever she wants to wear (as long as it is weather-appropriate). Even if she is wearing a green skirt with stripes, a purple shirt with checks, and pink shoes, **don't** say a word. Let your child use this form of self-expression. It will make her feel good about herself. Even compliment her on the way she looks. This will also aid in your child's self-esteem.

Manipulation is a way to test boundaries. It's important to set **your** limits and remember to keep your cool. Listen to your child's requests, assess each one, and always try to:

1. Set restrictions (they can't stay up more than ten additional minutes).

2. Know exactly what you are willing to give in on.

3. Use "Time-Out" (especially when the choices are not obeyed or your child keeps nagging).

4. Give specific choices (not more than two a day for younger children).

TANTRUMS

Sara, the mother of three-year-old Annie, was in a busy Los Angeles shopping mall. They had gone in one store after another. They walked by a toy store, and Annie had decided she wanted a toy. Sara said "no." But Annie was insistent. She began to whine and then cry. Sara tried to calm her. Then like a dam finally breaking, Annie sat down on the floor and started screaming, crying, and pounding. She was out of control—in the midst of an all-out, full-blown tantrum.

Sara was beside herself. This frantic child couldn't be her sweet, adorable Annie. Why was she doing this? Busy shoppers walked by and stared. Sara considered walking away but opted to wait it out until the fires burned down. This nightmare was to occur many times again before Annie's fifth birthday. Sara thought she had a troubled child. But in reality, she had a bright, normal child with a strong-willed, temperamentally difficult personality.

Children who have temper tantrums are not always problem children. It is important to assess how often and how severe children's tantrums are and if your child acts out physically toward others. If a child has tantrums many times a day, then it may be necessary to seek additional help. But a periodic tantrum, or even weekly ones, can be dealt with. Often, the parent can contribute toward the tantrum by pushing her child past her limits.

Temperamentally difficult children, besides being tantrum prone, can be argumentative and noncompliant. One of the most important points to remember related to tantrum-prone children is that they act out in order to stop parental directions or to simply get their own way. When Sara started to go into yet another store, Annie had a tantrum. Sara ceased her shopping and gave in to Annie's demands to leave. Sara, frustrated and embarrassed, started yelling at Annie, who finally stopped screaming and crying. Because Sara's yelling worked, it reinforced her behavior, which paralleled her daughter's.

Both behaviors (Sara's and Annie's) fed into a negative interchange. Both mother and child were left feeling angry, frustrated, and unloving. The way a family interacts together, their "family fit," has a lot to do with child temperament. We are not saying that if you are highly charged that your children will be highly charged or that that is necessarily bad. If your family functions **well** under charged circumstances, then the fit is right.

Tantrum Traits

Points to remember:

- **Do not** push a child past her physical or emotional limits.

- **Do not** respond with the same negative or aversive behavior as your child.

- **Do** remain calm.

- If your child is being disciplined and throws a tantrum, follow through with "Time-Out" until the tantrum is over.

- Your child is born with inherited temperamental traits. Understand your family fit and strive toward less family conflict and more cohesion.

"BRAT ATTACKS"

The first time your child says "no" you might find it rather cute, but wait and see how cute it seems after the tenth, twentieth, or fiftieth times.

As your toddler becomes more proficient in the use of language, you might be surprised to hear her talk back or argue with you when you give her a task to do or tell her "no." To many parents, sassy kids send up red flags, especially when parents are in public with their child. If your little three-year-old says, "Get out of my way. I don't like you," in a crowded mall, and some lady turns her head and mumbles under her breath, "What a brat," you might want to hang the kid on a clothes rack and leave her there for good.

Yelling at and spanking your child will only make matters worse. Can you imagine a three-year-old child and a parent standing and arguing with each other? Unfortunately, it happens all too often when parents do not know the "Time-Out" technique.

Sometimes, if the sassy talk is mild and you feel that your child is trying to assert her independence, it is better to **ignore** her. Usually children will talk back to gain attention. So it is best not to give them any when they are acting out.

Probably the best way to handle "brat attacks" is to teach your child what is acceptable and nonacceptable language and to praise her when she is being courteous and using good manners. If your child does not use acceptable language and you feel she has gone too far, immediately use "Time-Out." Children at this age often will engage in "toilet talk." This is normal. Do not react with horror. Simply ignore it, or you child will delight in your shocked attitude.

WHINING

Whining is **very** annoying. It can drive parents crazy. Nagging and whining can be constant, aggravating, and often lead parents to either scream or give in (both inappropriate responses). It is best to let children know ahead of time that whining will not be tolerated, and if it continues, the child will be put in "Time-Out."

For some children whining becomes a habit. Instead of talking, they whine. You can ignore a whiny child if she is tired, hungry, or hurt. It is best to assess if the whining is appropriate. If, however, you feel yourself getting frustrated after you have attended to your child's needs, then give one warning, and if she continues, use "Time-Out."

If you are in a situation that you cannot immediately change—for instance, if your child is hot and tired and wants to leave a place but you are unable to go—you should try your best to make your child comfortable. Maybe let her lie down on your lap. Get her a cool towel or washcloth. Buy some cold drinks.

Explain to children over four that "Mom or Dad is doing her/his best, and this is the way it is right now. Let's make the very best of our day."

Give your child **lots** of praise for trying to adapt to an uncomfortable situation. If your child helps the situation—for example, if she sits quietly, helps Mom with the cold drinks, lies down, and so on—, then reward your child when you get home or sooner if possible. Anyway use lots of verbal praise.

If your child whines for no reason, **ignore** her. Often children whine for attention. You can say, "I'm sorry, but I can't hear you when you whine. If you talk in a nice voice, I will listen." Children will often stop when they realize they can't get their way. If you can, leave the room when the whining starts. If it continues, use "Time-Out."

Listening

Many children whine because parents do not listen. They pretend to listen and will often pacify their children by saying, "I hear you," but they don't, and their child knows it. If you are preoccupied, tell your child, "Mommy or Daddy can't listen now, but I will when I am off the phone."

Active listening is when you attend to what your

child is saying by paraphrasing back what your child just said in words they can understand. By doing this, your child gets the message that not only did you **hear** her, but that you acknowledged her feelings. This is extremely important because:

- It allows your child to express feelings appropriately, as opposed to hitting or screaming or throwing things to get attention or vent emotion.

- It validates that talking about feelings is an acceptable way of expressing yourself when you're angry or hurt or depressed or sad.

- It teaches your child to seek social support from people she trusts when she is upset.

For instance, all the little boys at school were playing Ninja Turtles, and because Eric had not seen the movie yet, they excluded him. When he came home, Eric was still hurt and feeling rejected. Eric's mom sat down with him and said, "Eric, what's wrong? Tell Mommy what you are feeling." After actively listening to Eric, his mom said, "It hurt your feelings when your friends wouldn't play Ninja Turtles with you. Is that right?" Eric responded with a slight nod. After a big understanding hug, Eric and his mom made plans to see the Ninja Turtles movie that weekend.

When listening to your child:

- Look at your child eye-to-eye.
- Repeat what she said or asked.

- Let her express her thoughts even if you disagree.

- Don't interrupt her.

- Ask her questions.

If you do start to listen to your child, not only will you be amazed at all the interesting things she has to say, but you will discover that the whining, which was an attempt to get your attention, will subside.

The Parents' Part

Parents often promote whining without realizing it. Certain parenting styles inadvertently cause children to automatically resort to whining.

- **Tough love.** Some parents never like to give in to their child's requests. Thus, the child is frustrated and uses whining as a way of breaking the parent down.

- **Perfect Kids.** Parents often impose unrealistic expectations on small children. They expect them to perform tasks that are age-inappropriate, like asking a three-year-old to fold and put away her clothes.

- **The Love Smotherer.** Giving your children too much can encourage whining. Some parents create dependent, whining children by coming to their aid every minute. The child knows that she can get what she wants by whining, and it becomes an effective tool for the child.

- **The Guilt Tripper.** Many parents who do not

spend a lot of time with their children are easy targets. They feel guilty, the child picks up on this, and to mollify his or her own guilt the parent will give in to the child's whining.

Remember: Spend a lot of time actively listening to your child, and "Time-Out" your child when whining continues beyond your tolerance point. By combining "Time-Out" for whining with lots of positive attention when your child is talking, you will find that the time spent with your child is more pleasant for both of you.

8

The Sibling Solution

"He did it! She did it! She started it! It's mine!" If this is a familiar song in your home, perhaps you should tack the sibling solution chapter to your refrigerator.

One child can be a challenge. Two or more children often qualify parents for wartime medals. The first child is the sole attention-getter. This numero uno little being becomes your "miracle." The child becomes totally self-absorbed and begins to believe that the world really does belong only to her and that Mommy and Daddy are there to service her needs moment by moment.

Then out of nowhere the shock happens. Mom has announced a brother or sister is on the way. To a toddler this seems great in theory. They'll have a real baby instead of a doll to play with, and they can give it a bottle and help change its diapers. They can even help name the sibling.

The toddler doesn't realize that this sibling will get *a lot* of attention from Mom and Dad. They'll have to share time, perhaps their room, and maybe even someday their precious toys. When this phenomenon occurs, the sibling loses some favor. After all, life was great before the baby arrived. So, send him back to where he came from because the fun is over.

HOW TO LOVE THE NEW SIBLING

Toddlers are usually extremely excited at the idea of a new sibling until the sibling arrives. The cute little bundle is not visiting. It's home to stay and intrude on the space of Toddler Number 1 and the space of parents. This was not part of the bargain. As important as it is to make sure that your toddler gets lots of attention and feels loved, it doesn't mean that discipline, specifically "Time-Out," be forgotten when the new baby arrives. In fact, Toddler Number 1 will test the limits now, trying to direct attention away from the baby.

Establish rules regarding the new sibling before you bring the baby home. No hitting, screaming, pushing, or biting. If your child breaks any of these rules, put him in "Time-Out." No exceptions! Make sure your child feels like a helper with his sibling. Let him help you give the baby a bottle, change diapers, and rock the baby to sleep. Your toddler wants and needs to feel like he is a part of this new baby's life. This attitude will reinforce the concept of family. It will help your toddler start to feel protective of his new sibling.

It may be better to do your parental fawning over the newborn when your toddler is preoccupied. Program daily "special" time with Toddler Number 1 so he still feels loved and cared for. Otherwise, he will act out in order to get his share of your attention.

FIGHTING

Fighting is the most common problem among siblings. The parent becomes a chronic referee, and someone's feelings always end up being hurt.

Negotiation seems to be the only answer to sibling fights. If you set up a win-win situation as opposed to a win-lose situation, then everyone feels good. You want to avoid one child (maybe the instigator) feeling like the BAD child. This will label the child and cause only more angry interaction.

If you teach children how to resolve their own conflicts, then parents can start to step back from playing middleman. Usually parents will walk into a "hot fight" and end up hearing two screaming kids accuse each other of starting the fight. It's the old "he did it, she did it" routine. The communication breaks down, not only between parent and child, but between the siblings as well.

Sibling Conflicts/Fights and "Time-Out"

When you walk into the room and your children are already fighting, there is absolutely no way that you can truly find out who started the fight or conflict.

Because it takes two to have a fight or conflict, the only fair way to handle this situation is to "Time-Out" **both** children in separate parts of the home. Conversely, be sure to praise your children when they are playing together and interacting appropriately.

When your children are clearly fighting over a toy (thus not sharing), an alternative to sending them to "Time-Out" is to "Time-Out" the toy or game for the same amount of time. This teaches your children that by not sharing, they **both** lose access to the toy or game. Conversely, when your children are sharing and playing together appropriately, it's your signal to "catch 'em being good" and to praise them.

After "Time-Out," help your children find a solution to their argument by the following methods:

- **Express anger appropriately.** It is very important to help children know the difference between telling their sibling that they are angry and hitting them.

- **Give children words** to use so they can express anger properly. For instance, "I am really upset because you broke my toy," "Don't tease me, it hurts my feelings." These types of words will help your children vent their feelings without hurting one another. It is also a healthier way to express emotions. Words can and do leave emotional hurts. Children remember. By giving your children the correct verbal tools, they can maintain a positive relationship with their siblings.

- If your child does not respond, use "perspective-taking." Tell them to put themselves in their brother's or sister's place and try to feel what it is like to be treated in the same manner. For older children (five or older), this solution may work.

Remember to take into consideration the ages of your children when deciding how to handle sibling rivalry. Each child may have to be dealt with differently. You cannot discuss feelings at length with a three-year-old, but you can try to express in words for them the child's feelings. You can discuss with a seven-year-old his responsibility toward his younger sibling.

You may have to reinforce cooperative behavior many times and "Time-Out" fighting often. We have emphasized "Time-Out" and positive reinforcement throughout the book. These methods help a child develop good self-esteem and feelings of self-worth. When a child feels good about himself, he is more apt to be fair with others, because he does not feel as threatened by other children's actions. Children with good self-esteem are also willing to defend themselves when needed. Thus, always combine "Time-Out" for fighting with a lot of praise for playing together cooperatively.

9

Teaching Independent Play

PLAYING SOLO

One mother in the parenting class admitted, "The first time my daughter went to her room and was quiet for more than a half hour, I got nervous. I tiptoed down the hall and peeked into her room. To my amazement, she was playing by herself, and she was happy. How did this happen? For a year, I tried to get her to play alone, but she wanted company and attention all the time." The process of teaching independent play is a slow one. So when the miracle occurred, this mother was surprised.

She found that when she bought her child a toy that she could use in imaginative play, it greatly helped her extended concentration. In her case, she loved a toy house with small dolls and a car, bed, and swing. Each doll had a name and identity. She always had an activity to return to. Many young boys love trains, trucks, and outerspace scenarios. IMAGINATION is the key. Encourage a child to give their toys names, ages, and jobs.

There are times that you will want to help your child, which is fine—**once in a while**. But you must not solve every problem and teach them every game and how to use every toy. Your goal should be to try to encourage your child to function independently.

Children who learn to play well on their own are the ones who will play most successfully with other children and also feel more secure because they are able to amuse themselves and because they have acquired a sense of mastery over their environment.

Probably the most important aspect of independent play is that it prepares a child for dealing with problems. If you always bail your child out of situations, then they will forever be frustrated when someone is not there to help them.

Children, especially toddlers, are learning to impact their environment when they play. They learn what fits in the correct holes, and if it doesn't, then they are forced to revise their thinking. It's this revised thinking that creates the learning experience. This experience cannot be accomplished by parents or other children. **It can** only be done **solo**.

It is vitally important to begin working on independent play when the child is very young. An older child will know that she can get an adult to entertain her if she persists enough. These children may have trouble focusing on one activity, and this problem can spill over into their schoolwork. If parents constantly attend to their child, then the child will be less likely to use her imagination because her parents form her world.

When your child is playing by himself, even if it is for a few minutes, give him love pats and lots of verbal praise. Try to direct your child to an activity every night for a week and set the timer. Think of this as a game. Encourage your child to play until the timer rings. Gradually increase the timer by a minute or two every week. If your toddler throws a tantrum during this period, put him in "Time-Out."

PEER INTERACTION SKILLS

Parents often assume that all children play together naturally. But this is not necessarily true. Some children need a lot of supervision. The following steps will give you ways to help your child interact effectively:

1. You must have "catch 'em being good" and "Time-Out" well established before you begin to teach interaction skills.

2. Take the initiative and make play dates with other children. The first few times monitor your child carefully. Make sure you don't make other plans, as the children will keep you "beyond busy."

3. Don't plan a six-hour play date. One or two hours is **plenty**.

4. When your child is playing nicely, "catch 'em being good," and reinforce her good behavior.

5. Immediately use "Time-Out" for inappropriate behavior such as hitting, refusing to share, and so on.

6. If your child goes to "Time-Out," continue to play with her friend.

7. If your child has had trouble with peer interaction, have several play dates the first few weeks. Although this may totally exhaust you, the end result will be worth it—a socially adaptable child who can play independently. Make sure you monitor her play sessions.

8. Eventually, as your child learns to interact with other children, you will be able to let her play without your presence.

SLOW-TO-WARM-UP KIDS

Jamie thought four-year-old Erin was socially backward because every time she introduced her to a friend, Erin would retreat behind Jamie's skirt. Jamie was confused because Erin appeared so gregarious at home, but in public she was extremely introverted.

Some children are considered slow to warm up. This simply means that certain children need time to feel comfortable in new places with new people. You shouldn't force a child to say hello or to go somewhere that they are not comfortable, like a gym class or dance class. If you do take your child to classes, do not push her. Allow her to gradually join the group. Once she feels comfortable, she will make friends and enjoy the activity.

Gently encouraging your child to try new experiences, having friends over, and going to friends' houses to play all help your child explore "safe" situations during which she may feel some initial awkwardness. By gently encouraging her, however, you allow your child to gain valuable success in nonthreatening social situations, and with this growing sense of social competence, your child will gradually begin initiating contacts on her own. Remember, gently encourage, but don't push hard.

10

·

Parenting Conflicts

In the real world, there is not always a fairy-tale existence for children. There are more and more divorces, working parents, and "blended" families than ever before in our society.

For parents to continually help their children, they need to be aware that conflicts, either internally or with their spouse, can interfere with good parent-child interaction.

SINGLE PARENTS, DEPRESSION, AND MARITAL CONFLICT

Research has clearly shown that parental depression and marital conflict can separately and in combination have a profoundly negative impact on child behavior and psychological adjustment. There are several plausible explanations that in part account for the negative impact on children, explanations relevant to child-behavior management.

Specifically, there is growing evidence that depressed parents have **parenting styles** that may contribute to child-behavior problems. For example, research on parent–child interactions has shown that depressed parents display a higher proportion of negative, critical utterances toward their children, reinforce their children less, provide reinforcement and discipline in an indiscriminate or inconsistent manner, give vague or interrupted commands to which their children cannot comply, interact with their children with more critical and physically negative behaviors, and are less tolerant of their children's misbehavior. Taken together, the studies have indicated that depressed parents are more negative, hostile, and less reinforcing in their interactions with their children than nondepressed parents.

The research findings on marital conflict and parenting style essentially parallel the data on parental depression. Thus, the mechanisms by which parental depression and marital conflict negatively affect their child's behavior is explained in part by these **adverse parenting behaviors**.

What all this means for you as a parent is clear. In the early part of this book, we discussed the **problem-solving** approach to child behavior management. In this approach, we discussed identifying **the** problem first. It is important that you as a parent are sensitive to the fact that **your behavior** profoundly affects your child's behavior. If you find that you or your partner are depressed or are having marital difficulties, it is important to identify how this affects your behavior toward your child. As part of the problem-solving solution, you and your partner may need to seek professional help to deal with your depression and marital conflict first, before you can truly be consistent in your child-behavior management plan.

The following two checklists contain signs or symptoms often indicative of depression and marital discord. While not meant to be all-inclusive, if you find yourself experiencing some of these checklist warning signs, seriously consider seeking professional help for you and your family.

Realize that everyone feels sad or blue every so often or has disagreements and conflicts with his or her spouse. The difference between these rather normal feelings and disagreements and depression and marital disorder are matters of degree—that is, depression and marital discord are more intense, last longer, and significantly interfere with effective day-to-day functioning. The checklists are intended to help you begin to recognize some of the warning signs of depression and marital discord that can be a serious detriment to your attempts to effectively manage your child's behavior problem.

Signs of Depression Checklist

1. Depressed mood most of the day, nearly every day, experienced as feeling very sad and hopeless most of the time.
2. Markedly diminished interest or pleasure in all, or almost all activities most of the day, nearly every day—experienced as largely sitting around and doing nothing or engaging in mostly passive, solitary activities like watching television, eating, or napping. Going to work or doing daily household chores seems to require a tremendous effort. Everything seems like a chore, even social conversations.
3. Significant weight loss or weight gain when not dieting, or decrease or increase in appetite nearly every day, feeling almost always hungry or never hungry.
4. Insomnia, experienced as having trouble falling asleep at night, waking up repeatedly throughout the night, or waking up much earlier than you need to get up; or, in contrast, requiring much more sleep than usual nearly every day.
5. Feeling fatigued, lethargic, or a loss of energy nearly every day without an obvious explanation.
6. Feelings of worthlessness or excessive or inappropriate guilt nearly every day, experienced as a profound lack of self-esteem or excessive blame for all the troubles in your life and taking total responsibility for all your family's problems.
7. Diminished ability to think or concentrate, or indecisiveness nearly every day, experienced as difficulty keeping your mind on or completing work assignments or even everyday activities such as your checkbook, reading a book, or following a conversation. Making decisions and problem solving seem almost impossible or require tremendous effort.
8. Recurrent thoughts of death or that killing yourself would be an easy way to solve all your problems (this requires **immediate** professional help).

Signs of Marital Discord Checklist

1. Serious lack of communication experienced as spending too little time in talking, having nothing to talk about, always hasty or impatient conversations.

2. Always arguing over how to handle family finances—that is, too little, how it is spent, who manages it, and who earns it.

3. Always arguing over how to raise your children—for example, more discipline, less discipline, rules, too easy, too harsh.

4. Arguing over friends—for instance, not enough, too many, never doing anything with friends, always doing something with friends.

5. Arguing over recreation—such as, amount, kinds of, where to spend vacation or weekends.

6. Dissatisfaction with sex—for example, too little, too demanding, not sensitive to your needs.

7. Arguing over parents or in-laws—for instance, visit too often, not often enough, they are interfering in your life, don't help you financially.

8. Drug and alcohol interfering with daily family life.

9. Arguing over religion—perhaps, with which religion should the children be raised, or should they be raised with any religion at all.

10. Never or rarely showing affection toward each other.

11. Arguing or fighting in front of the children.

12. Regretting ever getting married.

13. Discussing separation or divorce with your spouse or with friends.

14. **Any** physical violence (this requires **immediate** professional help).

DIVORCED OR SEPARATED PARENTING

If you are a single parent, here are some general guidelines to help prevent a tough situation from being worse for your child:

1. Be certain not to fight or argue with your ex-partner in front of your child. Seeing his parents fight is a sure way of causing emotional and behavioral problems for your child.

2. Share this book with your ex-partner. It is very important that your child experience consistent child-management techniques from **both** parents.

3. Don't involve your child in conflicts with your ex-partner. This means don't use your child as a messenger between parents.

4. Seek professional help if you notice that you or your child are continuing to have an emotionally difficult time coping with the marriage separation or divorce.

WORKING MOMS

Many working mothers create a great deal of guilt for themselves. Not all women can be available on call 24 hours a day, become the president of the PTA, and drive daily car pools.

We all have a function in life. We all make choices. Whatever these are, whether by need or by desire, women, mothers, must accept and be proud to share their role with their children.

Problems arise when a young child detects that

his mother may have some discomfort with her role as a working mom. The child will manipulate his mother in order to get special favors, surprises, and excused from chores. Moms will often forgo "Time-Out" because they don't want to punish their child when they get home from work, because the time spent with them is often short.

But "Time-Out," and all of our rules of socialization, should be used with the same degree of consistency in all circumstances. It is important that your child's caregiver use "Time-Out" while you are gone. Many caregivers are reticent to do so, making the job of the working mother more difficult. You must convey to them the importance of using "Time-Out" and train them to use it. One mother had the "Time-Out" rules translated into Spanish for her live-in housekeeper. Another mother kept a "Time-Out" checklist on her refrigerator door. You may even want to have a practice "Time-Out" and go through the steps with the baby-sitter. If your child knows that there are no compromises because you work, he will be more apt to follow your rules when you are not at home.

It is also important not to bring your stress and problems from work into your house and transfer them onto your child. Your child deserves time with you when you get home, and you will need to put the phone calls and mail on hold unless there is an emergency. Give at least 20 minutes of uninterrupted "special playtime" to your child.

Share your work life with your children. Tell

them what kind of job Mommy has and what your office and workplace are like. Describe your job to your child. If possible, take your child with you one day for a short time and let him **see** where you work and meet your co-workers. Your child will feel a sense of belonging and security by being included in this very big and important part of your life.

If you work at home, set up rules and stick to them. Your child must understand that if you are constantly disturbed, he will be timed out. It is important that children start to respect your privacy at an early age.

Try not to get defensive if your little one asks you, "Why don't you bake cookies for school on Fridays?" Working mothers can add a dynamic and vital element to their child's life. You are a woman in the mainstream, contributing something to society and your family. As your child gets older, he will get a sense of pride from your contributions.

There are times when the emotions and guilt of working and not being able to participate in some areas of your child's life will overcome you. You may cry because you missed a school party or were not present for a swim lesson. Other nonworking parents may be judgmental, and this may hurt. But there is the choice—to work—and the reality—having to work.

Either one may put you in a push-pull existence. But staying at home and not working will not necessarily make you a better mother. The quality and depth of your caring and love is there, or it's not.

Although at three or four, your child may not comprehend this intellectually, he will emotionally. Be proud of who you are and so will your child. If you need to cry once in a while, go ahead. Even mothers get the blues.

11

"Time-Out" for Older Kids

POINTS, CHARTS, AND OLDER KIDS

As your child gets older, you may find that it is necessary to supplement the "Time-Out" procedure with additional behavioral techniques. Certainly by the time your child is eight or ten years of age, gradually introduce discipline techniques that are age-appropriate for older children, preteens, and teenagers. This chapter will provide a brief introduction to behavioral techniques for older children.

Setting up a point system can be a highly effective way to structure your parenting behavior. By using a point system with a chart, you will find that there is a clear structure or organization to providing positive reinforcement for behavior you want to increase, and corrective feedback (discipline) for behaviors you want to decrease. A simple chart can be set up as follows:

Behaviors to Increase or Decrease	Mon.	Tues.	Wed.	Thurs.	Fri.	Sat.	Sun.
Behavior 1:							
Behavior 2:							
Behavior 3:							
Behavior 4:							
Behavior 5:							
Daily Points:							
Total Week Points:							

WEEK BEGINNING: NAME:

Point Exchange: +1 = 15 cents; −1 = 10 minutes to bed earlier

Steps in Setting Up a Point System

1. Identify a behavior you want to increase (for example, do homework by 7:00 PM, clean up room by 6 PM, get ready by 7:15 AM for school bus).

2. Write the behaviors on the point chart and put the chart in a highly visible place (for instance, on the wall, bulletin board, or refrigerator door).

3. Select age-appropriate reinforcers (such as, one point equals 15 minutes television time, or ten cents, or ten minutes with computer game).

4. Complete the point chart every day.

5. Calculate points every day and weekly total

and exchange for backup rewards (or discipline).

6. Adjust backup rewards for points, depending on the success of the program.

7. Start the first week with one or two behaviors you want to increase, and then add additional behaviors after achieving initial success with the first behavior selected.

Examples of Behaviors to Increase with Points-Exchange Value

1. Be ready for school bus at 7 AM (+1 point).

2. Clean bedroom by 6 PM every day (+1 point).

3. Do homework by 7 PM every day (+2 points).

4. Sleep throughout the whole night without going into parents' bedroom (+1 point).

5. Didn't answer back the whole day (+2 points).

Since most behavior can be described either positively (that is, being on time for school bus) or negatively (late for school bus), it is much better to reward positive behavior that is incompatible with negative behavior (for instance, neat room versus messy room).

Each time your child earns a + (plus) point, provide a lot of praise and enthusiasm to socially reinforce the targeted positive behavior. If the behavior does not increase within one week, then decide whether the exchange reward is too little or the wrong selection. A good way to select a reinforcer is to see what your child normally does a lot (for example, plays computer games, listens to radio, watches television), and then make your child earn this activity on a daily basis with + points.

With all point systems it is essential that if you use money as a reward to be earned (for example, +1 = 10 cents), then your child should not receive a "free" allowance, but instead have to earn it with points. Otherwise, his motivation to earn points for positive behavior will be greatly decreased, because he is already receiving a weekly allowance.

At the end of the week, you can also provide a "weekly bonus" if your child has attained a certain number of points. For example, if your child could earn two points a day, and by the end of the week earns 12 out of 14 possible points, you might want to give a bonus two points for a "good effort" that week. This creates a positive family atmosphere and goes a long way toward making your interactions with your child much more pleasant and rewarding.

For younger children, instead of using + or − points, you can place smiley or sad faces or different color stars on the behavior chart to represent privileges earned or lost. Children as young as four or five years of age understand this simple system as long as you provide the backup reward or discipline shortly after posting the relevant face or different color stars.

Be certain **never** to take away + points that your child earns. This will only discourage your child and undermine the point system. Instead, either use "Time-Out" to decrease negative behavior, or use a − point system. For example, each time that your child answers back, she "earns" a − point, with each − point equal to 10 minutes to bed earlier or some other loss of privilege that is **separate** from the reinforcers earned by + points.

When the behavior you have selected is occurring at a level that is satisfactory to you, then you can gradually fade out the point system for that behavior by continuing to give praise and attention for the occurrence of the behavior, but giving points only every other day, then twice a week, then at the end of the week, and then not at all. If your social attention and weekly allowance is not enough to maintain the behavior, then reinstitute the point system.

School-Behavior Report Card

A point system can also be used to manage school-behavior problems such as acting out in class or other misbehaviors. You can set up a school-behavior report card with your child's teacher as follows:

1. Purchase three- by five-inch cards.
2. Write the behavior to decrease or increase at the top of the card.
3. Use a simple rating system such as:
   Circle one of the following:

   Unacceptable   Good   Very Good
       0   1   2
4. Have the teacher initial each card every day and send them home with your child.

5. If your child "forgets" or "loses" the card, then it's zero points.
6. Decide on reinforcers or discipline for points. For example, zero points equals "Time-Out" or to bed 15 minutes earlier that night, one point equals 15 minutes extra computer game time, two points equals 30 minutes extra computer game time or ten cents or some other relevant privilege.

A "TIME-OUT" ALTERNATIVE FOR OLDER KIDS

As children get older and approach adolescence, a viable alternative to "Time-Out" becomes necessary. The five-minute work chore technique is such an alternative. Begin by making a list of chores that will take about five minutes to complete. This can include such items as scrubbing the kitchen floor, vacuuming one room, polishing furniture, watering plants, washing dishes, cleaning a tub or shower. Also develop a list of longer work chores like washing the car, washing the outside windows, mowing the lawn, cleaning the inside of the oven. The procedures for the five-minute work chore technique are as follows:

1. Expect compliance to a command within 10 to 15 seconds.

2. If your child does not obey within that time, give **one** warning that you will assign a work chore if he does not start immediately.

3. Lack of compliance thereafter results in an assigned work chore.

4. After giving the work chore, monitor in an unobtrusive way that your child has started to do the chore.

5. If your child does not start the work chore after several minutes, warn **once** that you will assign an additional work chore if she does not begin immediately.

6. If your child continues to refuse to begin the work chore, then she is grounded for the rest of the day until she **completes** all ten minutes of the assigned work chores.

7. Being grounded means no privileges, that is, no television, telephone, computer games, stereo or radio, bike riding, skateboarding, outside social activities, no snacks, and no friends over. Until your child completes the work chores, she is to stay in her room with no privileges.

Be certain not to discuss the assignment after you have given it. Simply ground your child matter-of-factly, monitor her to make sure that she is not using anything that has been taken away (such as, the telephone or the stereo). In general, treat your child as if she has been timed out. When she completes the assigned work chores, she is then ungrounded.

12

·

Case Studies

·

The case examples in this chapter are composites of families seen by Dr. Varni in his clinical practice. While no one case is from a specific family, each represents a combination of actual experiences reported by the parents whose children are described. The examples are meant to show the wide variability in behavior problems seen, with some parents able to resolve their child's misbehavior rather easily and quickly, and other parents having a more difficult time, finding that their child's behavior problems will always be challenging as long as the child resides in the home. It is hoped that in these composites you as a parent will see some part of yourself and your child and have a clearer practical understanding of how to translate the principles set forth in this book into actual practice with your family.

CASE 1: TWO-AND-A-HALF-YEAR-OLD SANDRA

Two-and-a-half-year-old Sandra was described by her parents as "strong-willed, a discipline problem, won't listen, and a screamer." It had gotten to the point that Sandra's parents dreaded having other toddlers and their parents over to their house because Sandra's acting out would escalate during these visits. Both parents admitted to being soft touches when it came to disciplining Sandra, who was their first child after years of trying to have children. Typically, they would discipline Sandra for her behavior problem by sending her to her room for five to ten minutes, during which Sandra would scream and throw a temper tantrum. Then her parents would go into her bedroom to calm her down. Needless to say, this "discipline" proved to be highly effective in **maintaining** Sandra's behavior problem and illustrates the poor fit between a temperamentally difficult child and incorrect disciplining techniques. In fact, although Sandra had initially slept through the night, she had recently discovered that she could sleep in her parents' bed any night she chose by throwing a temper tantrum if her parents tried to return her to her room.

The first step in changing Sandra's behavior problem was to time her out whenever she acted out. Because both parents realized that Sandra was a temperamentally difficult child, they decided that a good time to start the "Time-Out" chair procedure would be over a weekend so that they could back each other up on what they anticipated would be a real battle for control. On Friday, they explained and then practiced the "Time-Out" procedure with Sandra, telling her that tomorrow (Saturday) they would be using the "Time-Out" chair in the hall instead of sending her to her room. Sandra seemed to understand but really was more interested in going back to her room to play with the many toys scattered throughout her bedroom floor.

The next morning, Sandra, being her usual demanding self, got "Time-Out" early in the morning. As soon as her mom said, " 'Time-Out' chair," the battle began. Sandra threw herself to the floor and started to have a temper tantrum. As calmly as she could, Sandra's mom stood her up, grasped her wrist, and with firm resolve, led Sandra to the "Time-Out" chair without saying a word. She sat Sandra down, walked away, and set the timer for two minutes. Well, as might be expected for a temperamentally difficult child, this first "Time-Out" was anything but two minutes! Sandra screamed and cried and yelled, and kicked and did all the behaviors that in the past resulted in her parents rushing to her side. This time it wasn't working, so Sandra upped the ante. She screamed louder, cried more vigorously, and finally resorted to "Mommy, Mommy, I won't do it anymore." This was **very** tough, but Sandra's mom stuck with it and waited to start the timer until Sandra was quiet, 47 minutes later!

By this time, Sandra was exhausted, her mom was emotionally drained, and her dad was wondering what they were doing wrong. Fortunately, even though Sandra made a few more halfhearted attempts at a scream or a kick during the two minute "Time-Out," she was quiet for the last 30 seconds, so her mom calmly (and exhaustedly) walked over and said in as pleasant a voice as she could, "OK, honey, you can get up now." At this point, "difficult" Sandra wanted a big hug from Mommy, and that's what she got. She had paid her dues, so it was more than all right.

Later that morning, Sandra's behavior again resulted in her mom putting her immediately into "Time-Out." This time, however, it took Sandra "only" 20 minutes to realize that being quiet got her out of the chair. When her dad timed her out that afternoon, after three other "Time-Outs" by her mom, Sandra was starting to get the message. The rules had changed. Now screaming and yelling weren't working like before. By the end of this first exhausting day, Sandra was still resisting somewhat in going to "Time-Out," but now after a minute or two of protest, she quickly quieted down and waited for the timer to go off. Because her parents stayed with it, and supported each other, they began the process of establishing their control over Sandra's behavior problem. Undoubtedly, being Sandra's parents would always be challenging, but now her parents had created a "good fit" between Sandra's difficult temperament and her family's style of discipline.

CASE 2: THREE-YEAR-OLD JEFF

Three-year-old Jeff was described by his parents as a "very normal child, maybe a little spoiled." Jeff's parents admitted that because Jeff was their first child, they had tended to dote on him, buying him lots of toys, spending all their time with him, and in general making him the center of their family. Naturally, Jeff loved all this attention, but was never satisfied, always wanting more parental attention and the latest toy or computer game he saw on television. While occasionally Jeff threw a temper tantrum when he didn't get his way, or said no a little more often than his parents would like, his behavior problems did not seem that bad because they almost always gave him everything he wanted.

Then disaster struck (for Jeff)! Into his rather idyllic life, Shari was born. Now, instead of being the center of his parents' universe, Jeff felt like he had been relegated to second string, last man on the bench. He didn't ask for a little sister, but here she was. Well, Jeff was determined to win his way back into the starting lineup. He was a star player, not a bench warmer!

In his attempts to regain his parents' sole attention, Jeff's behavior problems gradually increased in both frequency and intensity. By the time Shari was two months old, Jeff's parents felt it was time to talk to the pediatrician about Jeff's apparent sibling rivalry. Although the doctor assured Jeff's parents that this was normal, Jeff's behavior was becoming a real concern for his parents. Not only was he acting out a lot, but they were very unhappy that he did not share their joy over the baby. Because they insisted, the pediatrician referred them to the parent's group.

Fortunately, Jeff and Shari's parents caught the behavior problem very early. Combining "Time-Out" for temper tantrums, inappropriate attention-seeking behaviors (for example, touching the priceless vase on the end table), and other incidences of misbehavior, along with **a lot of attention** when he was being good, helping his mom feed the baby, gently kissing the baby, and generally being nice to the baby resulted in a dramatic decrease in Jeff's behavior problems. His parents made a point of spending "special time" with Jeff every day, reading him a story, and telling him how much they loved him. At the same time, they praised him often when he interacted positively with his baby sister and gave him a great deal of praise for acting like Shari's big brother. According to Jeff's parents, "Time-Out" was "really eloquently simple. It is sort of miraculous that it works so effectively! It's making parenting a lot easier!" Jeff no longer had to act out to get his parents' attention, and his parents now had a really viable way of handling the common behavior problems that are a normal part of young childhood.

CASE 3: FOUR-YEAR-OLD LISA

Lisa's parents described their four-year-old as having a bad attitude about everything—"She was always challenging authority." She'd get up in the morning, not want to get dressed, resist her mother's attempts to help her dress, and would eventually come down to the breakfast table "fussing and irritated." What a great way to start the day! Breakfast continued to be unpleasant, with Lisa never happy with **any** of the cereals offered her. Because she had selected every one of the nine or so cereals on trips to the supermarket with her parents, they were completely frustrated in their attempts to get her to eat a healthy breakfast. A jelly sandwich was not what they had in mind, but she **demanded** it every morning, and it was the only thing she would eat. "With the school ride almost here, who could argue!" To complete a "perfect" day, Lisa absolutely refused to go to bed by 8:30 PM. By the time her parents finished negotiating with her (for example, "I'll read you one more story, but then you have to go to bed!"), threatening, and anything else that seemed to get her to agree to go to bed, it was usually well past ten o'clock.

In further discussion with Lisa's parents, it became very apparent that the dressing, mealtime, and bedtime problems were all part of a larger behavior problem, that is, noncompliance. Lisa was the "tyrant-in-residence," defiantly resisting any of her parents' attempts to gain control over her behavior. Daily battles were part of the routine.

Lisa's parents set up a multicomponent behavioral program to deal with her many behavior problems. They used a four-minute "Time-Out" for any misbehavior that occurred during the day, such as refusing to do what she was told, answering back, and throwing temper tantrums. Although Lisa protested vehemently when the "Time-Out" chair was explained to her, somewhat surprisingly she offered little resistance the first time she was sent to "Time-Out" for noncompliance (not picking up her toys from the living room floor). The battle began, however, when she found out that after finishing "Time-Out," she still had to pick up her toys. After she was dragged to "Time-Out" two more times, Lisa finally picked up her toys. She definitely did not like going to "Time-Out," but after a few days she went without help.

For the bedtime, mealtime, and dressing behavior problems, Lisa's parents decided to combine a behavior chart with the specific behavioral techniques designed for each problem. On the chart, which was posted on the family's bulletin board in the kitchen, were listed four behaviors: Get dressed by 6:30 AM; eat breakfast by 6:50 AM; eat dinner within 30 minutes after starting; go to bed by 8:30 PM and stay there the whole night. For each behavior, Lisa's parents would set the timer to go off five minutes before the deadline, and then reset it to go off at the designated time. This gave Lisa a five-minute warning or grace period to complete the task. Each time she finished on time, she got a smiley face or a gold star on her behavior chart, accompanied by **a lot** of parental praise and attention. Each smiley face or gold star initially was exchanged for five minutes of "story-reading time," during which her parents would read her a story of her choice. Later, she could also "purchase" some small toys by exchanging her stars and faces.

In addition to the behavior chart, Lisa's parents followed the behavioral guidelines for bedtime, mealtime, and dressing behavior problems. For bedtime behavior problems, Lisa's parents started quiet time about 30 minutes before her 8:30 PM bedtime. During this time, Lisa went through a routine for dressing for bed, going to the bathroom, drinking a small glass of water if necessary, hearing a short story, getting hugs and kisses, and then being told good night. The first several nights Lisa got up after about a half hour, wanting some water, needing to go to the bathroom, asking for some more story time, and "kiss me, Mommy." Her parents, however, determined that this was all attention-seeking behavior, so without saying a word, they gently guided her back to bed. Later at night when she got up, they did let her have a few sips of water and go to the bathroom but, again, in a matter-of-fact, no-talking manner. They didn't want to accidentally give her attention for getting up, and they didn't! It took the better part of a week, but Lisa began to get to bed on time, stay there all night, and really seemed to enjoy all the praise and attention she got in the morning when she and her mom put the smiley face on the behavior chart.

For dressing behavior problems, Lisa's parents decided that she knew how to get dressed, but they had not established a good routine. The first step was to make certain that she didn't turn on the television set as she used to do. Then she was to get up, go to the bathroom, get dressed (matter-of-fact and to-be-expected attitude), and come down to breakfast. Lisa's parents got her up at 6 AM, which gave her 30 minutes to be ready in order to earn a gold star. The first couple of days her parents had to help her get dressed after the timer went off at 6:30 AM. But, Lisa quickly learned that it was more fun to get dressed before 6:30 and then come down to breakfast so she could watch *Sesame Street* on videotape for a longer time. Mealtime behavior problems were also handled more matter-of-factly. Lisa was given the choice of two breakfast cereals, that's all. The television set would stay on only as long as she was eating her cereal. She was given 20 minutes—an amount that her parents felt was sufficient. Dinner was the same. She was given small portions and no dessert until she had eaten her dinner. Any overt misbehavior resulted in "Time-Out." Lisa's parents made a real point of praising her for eating her healthy food and for finishing on time without acting out. Every time that she earned a smiley face or gold star, they made a big deal of it. It was hard work, but Lisa's parents reported that "she is really a lot happier now; she seems to want to be good; I can't believe how much more pleasant it is to be with her now!"

CASE 4: FIVE-AND-A-HALF-YEAR-OLD JASON

Five-and-a-half-year-old Jason was described by his parents as a "strong-willed kid who overreacts to everything. He screams, throws things, has temper tantrums, and in general is hard to control. He just doesn't listen. He always argues." Typically, Jason's parents would repeat themselves three or four times before yelling at him. Because yelling at him didn't always get him to obey or stop what he was doing wrong, they found themselves hitting him a lot more often than they wanted to. Afterward, they always felt guilty, but they didn't know what else to do. In contrast Jason's two-and-a-half-year-old brother, Brandon, was described by his parents as "sweet and even-tempered, an easy kid to raise." Yet, the sibling conflicts between the two brothers had grown so intense that Brandon was becoming more defiant in order to "get his share of the attention that Jason was getting for acting out." Although their parents suspected that Jason instigated a lot of the fights and arguments between the two boys, the brothers rarely started fighting when their parents were in the room. Rather, the parents would often hear screaming or yelling from the next room or a thump as the boys fell to the ground, hitting and kicking. By that time, it was all their parents could do to separate the boys, let alone try to figure out who started it. Jason and Brandon's parents were at their wit's end, frustrated by their lack of the happy and peaceful home life they envisioned and so desperately wanted for themselves and their sons. It was clearly time for outside help.

The first step involved explaining to the boys that from now on they would go into the "Time-Out" chair whenever they did not do what they were supposed to. During this family conference, each brother practiced the "Time-Out" chair. Brandon, as expected, was very serious and concerned as he practiced "Time-Out." He listened carefully to his parents' every word, and when they came to the part about getting one spank on his bottom if he got off the chair, Brandon looked at his parents with a furled brow and promised that he would not get out of the chair until the timer went off. In contrast, and true to character (temperament), Jason cavalierly went through the motions of "Time-Out," making certain that his parents understood that the chair didn't bother him. In fact, this was all rather a game to him. His parents, however, had been forewarned that some kids do this to undermine their parents' resolve to use the chair. Consequently, Jason's mother and father ignored his "I don't mind going into 'Time-Out'" attitude and instead made certain he understood what would happen if he got out of the chair. Finally, the brothers' parents explained that the next time they caught the boys fighting, both of them would be timed out in separate chairs in separate rooms. The parents made each brother repeat to them in his own words what would happen the next time they misbehaved and then smiled at both brothers and left the room.

Jason was the first brother to be timed out (no surprise!). Although his parents did not have to physically drag him to "Time-Out" by the wrist, he certainly made his mark on the way to the chair, using every expletive he had learned in his young life (sounding very much like his dad when he gets mad). He also threw in for good measure a few "I hate you" and "I don't care" comments. Although this hurt a lot, his parents stood their ground, looking firmly at him but not responding in any other way. As soon as Jason sat on the "Time-Out" chair, his parents went into the next room to set the timer. Bang! They never got to the timer. As soon as their backs were turned, Jason flipped over the "Time-Out" chair and was off! Fully expecting this to happen, his parents had agreed to begin "Time-Out" on a Saturday so that his dad could be around. Jason was a big kid, and his mom was not sure she could physically put him in "Time-Out" if he refused to go. So, in stepped Dad. He went to Jason's room where the boy had gone after leaving "Time-Out" and without saying a word, grabbed Jason by the hand and took him back to the chair. Jason pulled and screamed on the way, but his past experience had taught him not to hit his dad (because his dad would hit back, and hard! Although his dad did not like to hit Jason, out of frustration and anger, he hit him more often than he would have liked to admit).

Even though Jason sat back down on the "Time-Out" chair, it must have seemed like giving up this easy just wasn't right (he was like his dad in more than one way!). So after about a minute and a half, off he went again. This time, however, he was careful not to turn over the chair. Fortunately, his parents were monitoring him from the other room, so that within a few seconds his dad went into action once again. This time, Jason's dad grabbed him by the wrist and gave him one swift spank on his bottom. Jason felt this, even through his jeans, and fighting back his tears, sat in "Time-Out," this time for the full five minutes.

Jason tried getting out of the "Time-Out" chair later in the day when his mom timed him out, but went back with some struggle after his mom also used the one spank on the bottom technique. The rest of Saturday he stayed in the "Time-Out" chair, trying once on Sunday to escape. By the end of the weekend, Jason finally figured out that he **could avoid being spanked** if he would sit in "Time-Out" for five minutes. It began to seem like a good bargain, even though he really hated staring at the wall for **five whole minutes**!

Brandon got timed out only once on Saturday and twice on Sunday. Each time he sat there quietly, clearly hurt that he had done something wrong. Each time he sought a big hug afterward and said, "I'm sorry, Mommy," in a somewhat sobbing voice. He got timed out on Sunday a second time because he and Jason were fighting over their computer game. Both got timed out in separate rooms and spent the rest of Sunday playing together without fighting.

Although the boys still got timed out for fighting

after the weekend, the rate of fighting dropped dramatically, making for a much more peaceful home environment. Jason's still a difficult child to raise, but now his parents never hit him (he's learned to stay on the chair!), and they yell at him a lot less because they don't let his behavior escalate; they time him out as soon as he misbehaves. They always loved their son. Now they like him a lot more, too!

CASE 5: EIGHT-YEAR-OLD BRENT

Eight-year-old Brent's parents said he was "always testing to see how many times we have to ask him to do something, to see if we will eventually forget or just do it ourselves." Brent's behavior problem was clearly a high level of noncompliance to his parents' commands. His parents admitted that often they would get so tired of asking him to do something, like a house chore, that they would simply give up and do it themselves. In effect, Brent's parents had nicely set up a powerful reinforcement system for Brent's noncompliance. All he had to do was be defiant enough, and they would do it for him!

The plan for improving Brent's compliance to his parents' requests involved two components: An eight-minute "Time-Out" chair was implemented for noncompliance. Brent's parents were instructed to give him a command **once**, and if he did not start on his way within ten seconds, to then time him out. For routine chores around the house, a point system was set up. Using the behavior chart, his parents listed in very concrete and specific terms those chores he was to do around the house. These included taking out the trash every night before 6 PM (+ 1 point), feeding the dog after school every day and before 4:30 PM (+ 1 point), sweeping the leaves off the patio on Tuesday and Thursday (+ 2 points each time), watering the lawn daily (+ 1 point). Because Brent was getting a $5 a week allowance already as a freebie, his parents now required that he earn it through the point system. Because he could earn up to +25 points every week, his parents divided $5 by +25 points to arrive at 20 cents for each +1 point. His parents also had a category called "extra chores" on the behavior chart, which was a way for Brent to earn extra points (and money) **after** he completed his assigned chores for the day. Not surprising, this resulted in Brent offering to do additional chores! The extra dollar or so per week was well worth it to his parents to now have a son who actually did his chores, and then some.

CASE 6: NINE-YEAR-OLD KELLY

Kelly's parents considered their nine-year-old daughter "highly manipulative, always pitting us against each other in order to get her own way." To make matters worse, it seemed to her parents that her five-year-old brother, Mark, was learning how to drive a wedge between them as well by "seeing Kelly do it to us." Kelly and Mark's parents often disagreed on how to discipline their children. To make matters worse, they did not have these disagreements "behind closed doors," but argued rather vigorously in front of their children, not only on discipline but also on matters dealing with conflicts over finances and the state of their marital relationship.

From the beginning of the behavioral program, the children's father refused to take part. He typically preferred to let the children have their own way to avoid further conflict, or he would yell and scream, and occasionally hit, if their fighting and arguing got too loud for him. When the children's mother attempted to time them out for noncompliance, it was not uncommon for the father to interfere, saying, "Why are you starting, why are you starting? Why don't you just leave it alone?" Finding herself surrounded in the home with undisciplined children and an unsupportive husband, the children's mother progressively felt herself becoming more depressed. The negative-behavior cycle seemed to escalate with time, with her growing depression undermining her ability to use "Time-Out" effectively. Instead, she would scream and yell at the children and then simply give up. Marital conflict was also negatively affected, with her feeling more and more that she could no longer tolerate her husband's emotional distance.

Unfortunately, this was a family in serious trouble. The children's "behavior problems" were only one part of a much larger family issue. Consequently, family therapy was required to deal not only with the children's behavior problems, but also with marital discord and maternal depression. The family continues in therapy, and it will be a long time before they achieve a happier family life.

CASE 7: TEN-YEAR-OLD BRIAN

Ten-year-old Brian was described by his parents as "a problem, both at home and school." It was not uncommon for Brian to be sent to the principal's office at his school for fighting on the play yard or being disruptive during class. At home, his parents reported that Brian was always a difficult child to raise, even when he was an infant. They found themselves repeating commands several times, finally yelling and threatening to punish him for a week or more. Unfortunately, they would take away his privileges for such a long period of time (more than a month) that eventually they would give up on the punishment. Thus, Brian's parents did not have an effective way of disciplining Brian, and his behavior at home and school showed it.

Brian's parents decided that they would rather use the five-minute work chore technique than "Time-Out" in a chair for ten minutes. Every time Brian was noncompliant, answered back, swore, or engaged in any of the identified behavior problems, he was assigned a work chore. Initially, he resisted, but his parents stayed with it, grounding him for the day if he did not do his work chore. As opposed to the past, now Brian's parents truly grounded him by removing all privileges for the day, and they stuck to it! After being grounded for most of the day with no relief in sight, Brian finally completed the two work chores and immediately was ungrounded.

To gain some control over his school behavior problems, Brian's parents worked with his teachers and set up a school-behavior report card system on three-by-five-inch cards. Each day Brian's parents were given a rating of his overall behavior as Unacceptable (0 points), Good (+1 point), or Very Good (+2 points). Each time he received an unacceptable rating, he was immediately given a ten-minute work chore when he got home. Each +1 point was equal to a quarter. If he "forgot" to bring home the card, he got a ten-minute work chore that day.

Gradually, Brian's behavior began to change. His parents noticed a much more positive attitude. He seemed to like himself better as he stopped getting into trouble so often at home and school. He very rarely gets sent to the principal's office, and now his parents seldom yell at him. Brian's self-esteem has improved dramatically, and he is even trying harder at school now. It is important to note that his parents have also provided more structure for him in regards to studying and grades. When he comes home after school, he gets a snack and a maximum of one hour of television, computer games, or telephone time. Then, everything goes off, and he has to complete his homework and show it to his parents before he can watch television again for the night, or play with his computer, or talk on the telephone. Additionally, his parents have set up a point system for school tests. Each A = +4 points; B = +3 points; and C = +1 point. Each +1 point equals twenty-five cents. Slowly, ever so slowly, Brian's grades are starting to improve, and this also has enhanced his self-esteem. The older that children are, the harder it is to change their behavior, but Brian's really trying now, and his parents are supporting his progress every step of the way.

13

•

Questions and Answers

•

Question 1: What's the difference between a bad mood and bad behavior? Every time my little girl gets grumpy and irritable, she says, "I'm in a bad mood."

Answer: There's **no** difference between bad mood and bad behavior. You simply have not defined precisely enough what behaviors she is engaging in when you define her as being in a bad mood. Typically, parents find that when their child is in a bad mood, he or she is disobedient, defiant, resistant to instructions, answers back, and may throw a temper tantrum. "Time-Out" these behaviors, and forget about the "bad mood." Also, realize that your child has probably learned the excuse of bad mood for her bad behavior from you. Parents often accidentally model behaviors that come back to haunt them. Next time you come home in a bad mood or wake up in one and use it as an excuse for not being loving, or for ignoring your child, or for yelling at her, realize that your child is learning by observing you. If this is the case, it's time to stop and think and to problem solve **your** behavior as well.

Question 2: Should I "Time-Out" my little boy for not picking up his toys? He's five years old.

Answer: Yes, he's old enough to be responsible for picking up his toys. After all, he's the one who most likely put them all over the room in the first place. Simply tell him that you are going to set the timer for five minutes, and that he will get timed out if his toys are not picked up. Be sure to give him a lot of praise when he does pick up all of his toys. Remember, **"catch 'em being good!"**

Question 3: Every time I call home from the office and talk to my four-year-old, she whines and cries. How should I handle this?

Answer: There's probably no doubt that you feel very guilty when this happens. That's understandable. But, spending a lot of time on the phone trying to comfort your child will only reinforce her whining and crying. Tough as it may seem, you need to say to her, "Mommy will call back after you stop crying and whining." Then, **do call back** in ten minutes and be really upbeat if she's talking to you without crying or whining. Also spend a lot of time with her when you come home from the office. When parents work, their children **need** to spend a lot of time with them when they come home from the office.

Question 4: How old should a child be before you use "Time-Out?" I have an eighteen-month-old who's a terror.

Answer: Children as young as nine months old can be timed out with a modified procedure. When children under twenty-four months misbehave (for example, tantrums or hitting), simply say, "No!" Then pick them up and place them in the corner of a carpeted room and walk away. Don't worry if they don't stay there the whole minute or two. The idea at this age is that you have taken them away from what they were doing, while at the same time preparing them to take a "Time-Out" in the corner on a chair as a normal part of their lives as they get older. If it becomes apparent that this brief form of "Time-Out" is not having an effect, however, then remove all the toys from your child's playpen, and time him out in there for a minute or two when he needs discipline. Be sure he is quiet for a few seconds before taking him out of his playpen. After "Time-Out," simply pick him up from his playpen without saying anything and then place him on the floor among his toys. He's paid his dues, so now **"catch 'em being good!"** Remember, no yelling, spanking, or shouting at your child for misbehavior. Simply use "Time-Out" in a matter-of-fact way and provide him with a lot of praise when he's good.

Question 5: My son didn't listen to me after I asked him four times to do something. Finally, I called "Time-Out." He **begged** me not to put him in "Time-Out" and promised he would listen. I said

OK and didn't put him in "Time-Out." Was this wrong?

Answer: Most definitely yes, it was wrong. Children are notoriously clever and persistent in finding ways to avoid "Time-Out." You **must ignore** all such statements and matter-of-factly put your child in "Time-Out" without a word. Remember, each time you allow your child to escape from being timed out, you guarantee that the next time you attempt to "Time-Out" your child for a behavior problem you will have a greater battle getting him to go. Guaranteed!

Question 6: I saw my four-year-old son hit his seven-year-old brother. I put him in "Time-Out." Then, later the younger boy said that his brother hit him, but the seven-year-old denied it. What should I do?

Answer: Generally, the best policy is to "Time-Out" both children for fighting **that you see and not to accept verbal reports** from either child about who started hitting first. It is probably rare that you will accidentally walk into a room just as one child is hitting the other child. More typically, you will go into the room where your children are playing after you hear them fighting. In that case, just realize that you can't really know who started it, so assume that it takes two to fight, that they both are contributing participants, and then simply "Time-Out" both children for fighting. Only when you are **absolutely** certain that one child started the fight **unprovoked** should you ever "Time-Out" only one child. This is typically not the case, so you should probably "Time-Out" both children the vast majority of the time. Also, it is wise not to "Time-Out" a child based on the verbal statements of a sibling that he hit her. If you didn't see it, you shouldn't time a child out for hitting. In the long run, it is better to "Time-Out" all incidences of **observed** fighting than to potentially unfairly "Time-Out" a child who really did not hit a sibling.

Question 7: If my child is overtired and cranky at the end of the day, and she misbehaves, should I still put her in "Time-Out."

Answer: Prevention can often be the best cure for this problem. Problem solve why your child is so tired. Is it because she is not going to bed early enough? Does she need a midday nap? Is she eating adequately? Did she play too hard? When you can identify the cause of your child's tiredness, then make plans to avoid these situations in the future. Misbehavior must be timed out when it occurs, however, or you run the risk of gradually slipping back to inconsistent discipline, and consequently you'll find yourself with a reoccurring behavior problem. Besides, if your child is truly tired, sitting in the "Time-Out" chair is better physically than running around the house being cranky and getting into trouble.

Question 8: My five-year-old daughter will be naughty, and just as I tell her to go to "Time-Out," she says, "Oh, Mommy, I love you so much. Please don't put me in 'Time-Out,' " or she'll do something funny or cute. I'm not getting very far.

Answer: First, be as matter-of-fact as possible, and then **put your child in "Time-Out" no matter what she says!** You can say, "Mommy loves you, too, but now you have to go to 'Time-Out' for what you did." Then, don't say another word. If she does something funny or cute, try not to respond—no matter how hard it seems. These are all manipulative actions by your daughter in her attempts to avoid "Time-Out." Don't give in. Be strong! Anytime you allow her to escape "Time-Out" you are accidentally reinforcing manipulative behavior and simultaneously not disciplining her for her behavior problem. The long-term outcome is pretty unpleasant.

Question 9: How do you handle sassy back talk?
Answer: First, very specifically define to your child that what he just said was unacceptable behavior because it is impolite and disrespectful. Tell him the next time he talks to you this way, you will time him out. If he continues, then immediately put him in "Time-Out." If the back talk does not bother you, then simply ignore it, and do not reinforce the behavior by giving your child your attention. "Time-Out" will stop the sassy back talk pretty quickly. Ignoring it will take a lot longer.

Question 10: Should I use "Time-Out" if someone else tells me that my child was bad?

Answer: The answer to this question depends on the source. If your child's teacher or a good friend of yours, whose perception of your child you trust, reports to you that your child misbehaved, then you should believe the veracity of their statement. Always consider the source, however. You may or may not want to discipline your child based on the statements of a neighbor or another child's parent if you are uncertain of their ability to tell you all the facts. If you believe that your child did misbehave when he was with someone else and that it was the **first time** it occurred, warn him that next time he will be timed out when he gets home. This may be sufficient. If the misbehavior was serious, however, or if it has happened before, your child should be timed out **and** sent to bed earlier that night (or no television or other loss of privileges) to underscore the fact that his misbehavior with others is not to be tolerated.

Question 11: My friend will not "Time-Out" her child for bad behavior. So when our kids play together and I "Time-Out" my little boy, he gets upset that his friend gets away with so much.

Answer: Children will always compare themselves to other children, including how their friends are disciplined by their parents. Simply respond with the same statement, "That's fine for Billy's family, but this is how our family does things." You can't control how other parents discipline or don't discipline their children. So don't even try. Just do what you now know is the best way to discipline your child.

Question 12: My seven-year-old son, Noah, will not go to "Time-Out." Even when I ground him until he does his "Time-Out," he just continues to do what he wants. I know that he doesn't like to go to bed earlier and that he will go into "Time-Out" when his dad comes home. How can I get him into "Time-Out" without waiting for his dad to come home? It's just not fair to hit Jack with conflict as soon as he walks in the door after a hard day at his office.

Answer: First of all, make certain to problem solve that you are using "Time-Out" correctly. Then, be sure not to engage in verbal discussion and arguments with your son over going to "Time-Out." Simply say, "That's 'Time-Out' for seven minutes." If he does not go to "Time-Out" within 10 to 15 seconds, say, "If you don't go right now, you're grounded for the rest of the day until you do your 'Time-Out,'" and then walk away. You should have explained to him previously what grounding means, so monitor him for any infraction of the rules. If you catch him breaking the grounding rules, say, "That's fifteen minutes to bed earlier tonight." Mark down each time you add another 15 minutes. If he goes into "Time-Out" before his dad comes home, he's off grounding and can go to bed at his regular time. If he doesn't go to "Time-Out" until his dad comes home, then after serving his "Time-Out," he's off grounding but still has to go to bed earlier based on the amount of time he lost by not following the grounding rules (for instance, 15 minutes × 4 = 60 minutes to bed earlier). Because Dad is home at night, you shouldn't have any trouble getting him to bed earlier. Additionally, now that he knows that you have so many backup options, he should quickly start serving his "Time-Out" time, because the cost has gotten too high not to.

Question 13: Why do children dislike "Time-Out" so much?

Answer: The answer is relatively simple: It's incredibly boring! Try it yourself for ten minutes, and you will find that staring at a blank wall is very aversive. Children constantly need visual stimulation. That's why television gets watched so much. Sitting and staring at a blank wall is aversive, but if done correctly, it does not carry the emotional baggage that comes with yelling at your child. "Time-Out" provides highly effective corrective feedback without hurting your child emotionally. That's why it works!

Question 14: What do I do if my eight-year-old son swears at me and knocks over things with his fist on the way to "Time-Out?" Also, when he's in "Time-Out," he swears at me, calls me names, and occasionally kicks the walls. What do I do?

Answer: Sit down with your son during a calm time and explain to him that **each** time he swears at you or knocks over things on the way to "Time-Out" you will add another minute to his eight minutes. Also, explain that when he swears, calls you a name, or kicks the wall when in "Time-Out," that you will **reset** the timer to eight minutes plus any additional minutes he "earned" on the way to "Time-Out." Remember, you should discuss this with him before your next "Time-Out." When you are timing him out, add the extra minutes **without saying a word**. Otherwise, your reaction will accidentally reinforce his swearing and actions. The same is true when he's in "Time-Out" and calls you a name, swears, or kicks the walls. Just reset the time to eight minutes plus any additional minutes without saying a word. He'll eventually get the message that it's just not worth it to swear and kick!

Question 15: What prevents some parents from disciplining their children or hesitating to discipline them?

Answer: There are a number of reasons why a parent might not discipline their child. For parents who do not know of the "Time-Out" procedure, their typical discipline includes a lot of yelling, some hitting, and removal of privileges. Hitting and removal of privileges are usually saved for the "bigger" behavior problems, so most parents find themselves regularly yelling, threatening, and nagging their child to do what they are told. This is usually pretty aversive for the parents, so they'd rather "let things slide" or "do it myself" to avoid the hassle of disciplining. Some parents might not discipline, but instead try to cajole their child into compliance, because they were hit and yelled at as children, and they are making a real effort not to do the same to their child.

Even after some parents learn "Time-Out," they sometimes do not use it regularly because of the **perceived** greater effort required. Timing out their child for every behavior-problem occurrence seems like so much work. In reality, using "Time-Out" effectively eventually results in disciplining your child less as you gain better control over his behavior problem. **Frequent use of "Time-Out,"** without **yelling or hitting**, is the most therapeutic thing you can do for your child when it comes to discipline. It requires more upfront effort to change an existing behavior problem, but in the long run, it will actually be less work. **Use "Time-Out" often** without hitting and yelling, and both you and your child will be happier. As one little four-year-old girl pleaded to her daddy who apparently felt "Time-Out" was too much work and who incidentally would yell at his daughter after she continued to be disobedient, "Daddy, please don't yell at me. Put me in 'Time-Out' instead." Yelling is emotionally destructive to children. **Use "Time-Out" often!**

Question 16: My daughter demands so much of my attention even after I spend a lot of time with her. It can be so frustrating. After I've spent an hour or more playing and interacting positively, I tell her I need to get some chores done. She starts whining for more time with me. After a lot of her continued whining, I get frazzled and irritated and end up yelling at her to stop whining. She starts crying and I feel guilty! What can I do?

Answer: Children need to spend positive time with their parents, so make certain that on a daily basis you are setting aside enough time to be with your child. If you judge that you are doing so, then you need to put limits on your child's persistent whining by viewing it as a behavior problem. After spending sufficient time with your child, explain to her that "now Mommy has some work to do," and without a lot of fanfare, leave the room and go do your chores. If your child follows you and persists in whining, simply tell her in a calm voice that if she doesn't stop whining, you will have to put her in "Time-Out." If you do this without yelling, then you will not turn a pleasant time together into a fighting match. Matter-of-factly put her in "Time-Out," and gradually she will learn to enjoy the times together with you without having to demand more at the end by whining. Just do it every time that she whines, and do it without yelling or nagging at her to stop whining. Be consistent, don't yell or nag, use "Time-Out" every time, and it will work!

Question 17: What do I do when my seven-year-old stalls at night to avoid going to bed on time? I time him out if he persists. Is that OK? Also, should I still read him his story before lights out?

Answer: Timing him out for stalling is correct. Stalling should be viewed as noncompliance. But do not extend his bedtime in order to read him his story. Otherwise, you have just reinforced him for stalling, that is, he gets to stay up later after all when he finished his "Time-Out." Stick to the same bedtime every night, and read to him only until that time, then lights out.

14

When "Time-Out" Isn't Enough

WHEN TO SEEK PROFESSIONAL HELP

The focus of this book is on the common everyday behavior problems of childhood. In many ways, this is a self-help book for parents who want to make normal childhood conflicts more manageable and the time they spend with their child more enjoyable.

Yet, there are emotional and behavioral problems some children experience that require professional help. These emotional and behavioral problems differ from the common everyday behavior problems that respond to the techniques described in this book by the nature of their severity, intensity, frequency, and profound negative impact on the child and family.

When in doubt, even the slightest doubt, contact your child's pediatrician and set up an appointment. Most pediatricians know of mental health professionals (for example, pediatric psychologists, psychiatrists, marriage and family counselors, clinical social workers) in their community who are experts in child psychology. Ask for at least two referrals. This way, you can have a choice after talking to each professional. Not every mental health professional has the expertise to work with children's more severe emotional and behavioral problems. Be a smart consumer! Ask questions regarding their training experiences with other children with the same kind of problem, and how long they think it will take to help your child.

You may also want to supplement the referral names given to you by your pediatrician by asking other parents who have children the same age as your child. When you find a professional who helped a friend's child, then it may be worthwhile to also interview this individual. Remember, don't simply take your child to a mental health professional and assume that this individual is the most qualified person to help your child. Spend the time to be sure. Your child is too important to simply entrust him or her to any Ph.D., M.D., MFFC, or MSW in the neighborhood. Unfortunately, an advanced degree is no guarantee that a professional has been well trained to treat the particular emotional or behavioral problem your child is experiencing. Ask questions at all times, and if you are not satisfied with the answers, seek out another professional. The following are just **some** of the emotional and behavioral problems that are best managed with professional help:

- **Depression and severe social withdrawal.** Everybody, children and adults alike, experience the blues, temporary ups and downs. But, if you find that your child is exhibiting a prolonged pattern of depressed mood and withdrawal from social interactions, then contact your pediatrician immediately.

- **Attention deficit hyperactivity disorder.** Some behavior problems are simply too difficult to handle without professional help. Severe forms of acting-out behavior, temper tantrums, and the like, particularly when combined with impulsivity, short attention span, and high levels of overactivity, may be symptoms of attention-deficit hyperactivity disorder. Professional help is truly needed to deal with this challenging behavior problem.

- **Anxiety disorders.** Sometimes children develop fears or phobias that are so severe that they have a profound impact on the child's normal day-to-day existence. Some children may refuse to go to school because of anxiety, or may avoid other normal activities of daily living because of severe feelings of fear or anxiety. These emotional problems are more than the common separation anxieties of childhood and require professional guidance in order to treat them successfully.

These few examples are meant only as illustrations. The most important point to remember is this: **When in doubt, contact your child's pediatrician.**

Epilogue

— ■ —

Future Behavior Problems

— ■ —

PSYCHOLOGIST

With hope, by this time, you have had a number of successful experiences using the "Time-Out" procedure and other behavior techniques described in this book. As part of the problem-solving approach, it's time to plan for the future.

It is an inevitable part of the growing child that behavior changes over time, and problems solved today may reappear in a different way in the future. While a three-year-old may throw a temper tantrum by falling to the ground and kicking wildly, an eight-year-old may throw a temper tantrum by throwing his toys against the wall or swearing. In either case, you would still use "Time-Out."

It is essential to remind yourself often that your behavior is a major determinant of your child's behavior. With this in mind, you will come to realize that you can handle most future behavior problems by **first changing your behavior**. After more than 15 years of working with families, I have found that unfortunately when things are generally going well, it is the parents who first slip back to old incorrect discipline methods (for example, yelling or threatening), inevitably followed by their child's renewed behavior problems. Thus, change your behavior first, and most likely your child's behavior will follow. Remember, try to be consistent.

The important thing to keep in mind about future behavior problems is that you have the skills to deal with them by going through the problem-solving steps presented at the beginning of this book. If you ever doubt that you can solve a new behavior problem on your own, please be sure to contact professional help. Otherwise, take a deep breath, think about your problem-solving steps, and then try it out. You will probably be very pleased with the result.

PARENT

While I was writing this book, **I lived it**. Almost every chapter was experimental. Dr. Varni and I would sit together in writing sessions, and I ended up asking him 20 questions before we finished a chapter. Over the course of almost a year, I saw my child change and grow, and I tried to include my own "Time-Out" experiences in the book as a basis for helping other parents.

I was a bit cocky when I began writing, because

I thought I was a "Time-Out" expert. Now I see that "Time-Out," and all of the socialization techniques used in our book, are ground rules for my own learning process.

During this year, I made many mistakes. I became frustrated at one point and had to reread my own guidelines to get me back on track. But something clicked after a few months when I realized that even through frustrating times, I was now using "Time-Out" **consistently**.

That consistency is what worked. My child would continue to change, and I would have difficult times, but she knew her limits with me and what the outcome would be if she acted inappropriately.

I suppose my desire to write a second book with Dr. Varni about preteens and teenagers comes from a selfish, as well as an altruistic, place. I want to have all the tools ready for the time when my toddler becomes a teen. I'd like to have those tools to share with other parents, too.

There is something about a camaraderie of effort that makes even the most difficult situations more tolerable. I know that while I wrote and lived *Time-Out for Toddlers*, so did many of my friends. We were witnesses to one anothers' failures and successes, we constantly shared experiences, and we reminded one another of the rules.

Ultimately, the parents became my inspiration. I encourage all of them to continue using the methods in our book, not to lose faith in their effectiveness, and to hold tight while we get you ready for adolescence.

ABOUT THE AUTHORS

DR. JAMES WALTER VARNI is a Clinical Professor of Psychology and Pediatrics at the University of Southern California and Director of the Behavioral Pediatrics Program at Orthopaedic Hospital in Los Angeles as well as a clinical research consultant to the Department of Pediatrics at UCLA, Shriners Hospital for Crippled Children–Los Angeles Unit, and Miller Children's Hospital of Long Beach Memorial Medical Center.

Dr. Varni received his Ph.D. from the Department of Psychology at UCLA in 1976. He was a postdoctoral fellow in pediatric psychology in the Department of Pediatrics at the Johns Hopkins University School of Medicine in 1977. Dr. Varni is a fellow of the American Psychological Association and the Society of Behavioral Medicine. He has published more than 100 professional articles and book chapters on children and families and two professional books on behavioral pediatrics. In addition to an active pediatric clinical-research career, Dr. Varni also maintains a clinical practice in pediatric psychology. Dedicated to a scientist-practitioner philosophy, Dr. Varni strongly believes in applying research-generated cognitive-behavior therapy techniques to clinical practice on a timely basis. This is the philosophy for the genesis of *Time-Out for Toddlers*; state-of-the-art, scientific techniques applied to the clinical problems of children and families.

DONNA GELGUR CORWIN has been a writer for more than twelve years and has a Master of Arts degree from UCLA. She has written and published in excess of 100 articles on contemporary family issues, travel, and life-styles for such magazines as *L.A. Parent, Moxie, Savvy, GQ, Los Angeles Magazine, Shape, Slimmer, Motorland, Incentive Travel, LA Style,* and numerous others.

Ms. Corwin has been a guest travel-editor on the syndicated new show *The Parenting Network*, and a guest on *California Family*, a television show on KHJ in Los Angeles. She has also appeared on *Donahue* and *Hour Magazine*.

Ms. Corwin is a screenwriter and has written for numerous television shows as well as writing a screen adaptation of the book *A Wrinkle in Time* for producer Norman Lear.

She has written screenplays for a number of producers and is currently working on an original screenplay, *A Day for Heroes*, with best-selling author Syd Field. She has also created a half-hour television series for children, *Star Kids*, based on the Star Kids reward charts.

She is a member of the Writers Guild of America, Women in Film, Screen Actors Guild, and is included in the *Marquis Who's Who in American Women*. She is also a Vice President of the Neil Bogart Children's Cancer and AIDS Foundation.

Ms. Corwin resides in Beverly Hills with her husband, Stan Corwin, a publisher and producer, and their young daughter, Alexandra.